GOING ◆◆◆◆
TO THE SOURCES

GOING ◆◆◆◆ TO THE SOURCES

A Guide to Historical Research and Writing

Third Edition

ANTHONY BRUNDAGE
California State Polytechnic University, Pomona

HARLAN DAVIDSON, INC.
WHEELING, ILLINOIS 60090-6000

Except as permitted under United States copyright law, no part of this publication may be reproduced or distributed in any form or by any means, or stored in a database or any retrieval system, without prior written permission of the publisher. Address inquiries to Harlan Davidson, Inc., 773 Glenn Avenue, Wheeling, Illinois 60090-6000.

Library of Congress Cataloging-in-Publication Data

Brundage, Anthony, 1938–
    Going to the sources : a guide to historical research and writing / Anthony Brundage.—3rd ed.
        p. cm.
    Includes bibliographical references and index.
    ISBN 0-88295-969-7 (alk. paper)
        1. History—Methodology. 2. History—Research. 3. Historiography. 4. History—Research—Data processing. I. Title.

D16.B893 2002
907'.2–dc21

                                                2001051869

Cover illustration: "The Route of the Corps of Discovery to the Pacific" (the journey of Lewis and Clark), courtesy of Ken Burns and Florentine Films. Map art by Jane Domier.
Cover design: DePinto Graphic Design

Manufactured in the United States of America
06 05 04 2 3 4 TS

TO MY STUDENTS ◆◆◆◆

Contents ◆◆◆◆

Preface ◆◆◆◆

This book developed out of a course on History Methods that I have taught to upper-division history majors for many years. As anyone who has taught a methodology course can attest, it can be an either uniquely rewarding or deeply frustrating experience; usually it is both. Typically, students approach the course with some apprehension. Up to this point, their academic encounters with history have been chiefly in the form of lecture-discussion courses, a format with which they feel relatively secure. Suddenly, in the History Methods class they find themselves on unfamiliar terrain, confronted with new, sometimes perplexing challenges. Fortunately, often mingled with this feeling of apprehension is a sense of excitement about the prospect of achieving new levels of understanding of their chosen discipline as well as acquiring a new set of research and writing skills. It was in the hope of fostering the excitement, allaying the apprehension, and developing the skills that I undertook the writing of this book.

Central to my own sense of the excitement of history is an appreciation of it as open-ended and dynamic. Developing that awareness in others is an important source of satisfaction for me as a teacher of history. I have therefore structured my course and this book around the concept of history as a dynamic process. The common tendency to view history as fixed and static is best overcome by exploring the ways in which historians actually go about examining the past, constantly searching for fresh patterns and meanings, and developing new methodologies to achieve them. Accordingly, an introductory chapter on the history of history writing sets the stage for a discussion of the types of historical sources and the organization of the historical profession in Chapter Two.

Chapter Three, on how to locate your sources, is the central chapter as far as research methods are concerned. It is a detailed, practical guide through the various resources that enable you to identify and obtain the essential books, articles, essays, and other materials relating to your topic. Once this knowledge is acquired, the essential bibliography on any historical topic can be located readily. Fostering one's ability to operate as a competent, self-directed researcher is one of the major goals of this book.

Another major goal is to introduce the student to some of the fundamentals of writing history. Chapters Four and Five explore the methods of writing two common types of paper, the historiographic essay and the research paper. This follows the sequence of my own teaching, in which a historiographic essay (based chiefly on secondary sources) is the centerpiece of the History Methods class, while a longer research paper (using primary as well as secondary sources) is assigned in the Senior Thesis and Seminar. The concluding chapter recapitulates some of the major points made in the book, in particular the theme of the open-ended nature of history. The achievement of creative insights and analyses is shown to be closely linked to the concept of history as a dynamic intellectual discipline.

Online databases for historical researchers have improved enormously in recent years, as have college library gateways to these databases. Better access to a wider range of scholarly titles, and the increasing availability of full-text articles, required a major overhaul of those parts of *Going to the Sources* dealing with research. Internet searching also receives a more extended treatment. At the end of the book, new appendices provide easy-to-follow examples of formatting for both footnotes/endnotes and for bibliography entries. Another new appendix, on commonly used abbreviations found in scholarly works, should also prove helpful.

The student-authored historiographic essay in Chapter Four has been replaced by a very recent one. Unlike the previous specimen essay, this one is given in full, including introduction, conclusion, endnotes, and bibliography, with marginal notations pointing out the major parts of the essay. The subject of this new essay—how historians have approached and interpreted the Lewis and Clark Expedition—seems appropriate with the impending bicentennial of that great national enterprise. It is also a topic that resonates with the very nature of historical research and writing. While historians, unlike the members of the Corps of Discovery of 1804–1806, are not (usually) placed in physical peril, historical research at its best is driven by the same qualities of adventurousness, determination, and a passion to explore and explain the unknown. In revising this book, I have been assisted considerably by the suggestions of numerous faculty members around the country who have been using *Going to the Sources* in their classes. My wife, Martha, gave the manuscript a careful and critical reading. Kate Seifert, of the Reference, Instruction, and Collections Services of my university library, provided expert advice and many useful recommendations. I am greatly in their debt.

CHAPTER ONE

The Ever-Changing Shape and Texture of the Past

STATIC AND DYNAMIC CONCEPTS OF HISTORY

A recent cocktail party conversation made me acutely aware of some common misconceptions of my chosen field of study. After being introduced to a psychologist, I listened with keen interest to his enthusiastic account of some of the latest approaches and interpretations in his discipline. Having expostulated on this topic with obvious relish, he said, "I don't suppose there's much new going on in your field." Stunned by this remark, I scrutinized his face carefully for signs of either humor or intentional offense. Seeing neither, I was forced to conclude that he genuinely believed history to be a passive if not dormant discipline. I attempted to disabuse him of this unfortunate view by explaining some of the newer developments in recent decades in the field of history: social history, women's history, cliometrics, psychohistory, and postmodernism. The mention of psychohistory produced a detectable flash of interest, and I would like to think that he has since begun to question whether history is quite the fixed, dull chronicle he had imagined it to be.

Reflecting later on this encounter, I realized that my companion's attitude was by no means unusual, even among highly educated persons. The reasons for this are readily apparent. The popular conception of history as simply a record of past events seems to have as an obvious corollary history's basic unchangeability. History is often seen as a vast array of facts, largely political and military in character, arranged more or less chronologically. Thus conceived, history is viewed as unalterable except by the occasional unearthing of a lost city or the discovery of a trunk full of letters in an attic. At its best, it is an exciting and vivid costume drama; at its worst it becomes a tedious, turgid catalog of dates and names de-

1

signed to torment the young. We should not be surprised that it is the latter viewpoint that predominates. Not only is modern American culture remorselessly present-minded, but many times the way in which history is taught in our precollegiate schools only reconfirms its dull reputation.

Things tend to improve at the college level, where those who have not already developed an attitude of unremitting hostility toward history often discover that it offers them an exciting new set of intellectual challenges and vistas. Yet even at this level, introductory courses sometimes only solidify students' negative attitudes. It is not a question of bad teaching; knowledgeable, enthusiastic, and articulate history teachers abound at every level. The problem lies in presenting history as a story with a fixed plot and cast of characters. It is true that this approach is natural and to some extent unavoidable, particularly with students receiving their first systematic exposure to history. But it is also possible, indeed critically important, to offer at least a glimpse of a very different concept: history as a dynamic process. By this I mean a rich, varied, evolving intellectual system that allows us to achieve a deeper and better understanding of our world, indeed of ourselves. In this vein history still deals with the past, but it conceptualizes a past in constant dialog with an ever-advancing present, one that responds to new questions and reveals fresh insights into the human condition. This is history as it is understood (and enjoyed) by professional historians, and it is high time that others were let in on the secret.

Obviously, this concept of history stands in sharp contrast to the static one that prevails when we think of history merely as a fixed story. In the former the past becomes kaleidoscopic, offering different answers to each inquirer. This should not be taken to mean that every person can fashion whatever he or she wishes and call it history. There are rigorous procedures to be observed in the framing of historical questions, in the selection and interpretation of sources, and in the presentation of one's findings. Moreover, the pursuit of objectivity, though impossible to achieve fully, must always be a central concern of the historian. Not everyone finds the dynamic concept of history appealing; there is, after all, something comforting about the supposed unchangeability of the past. A shift from the static to the dynamic can be as disconcerting, as our recent (in terms of natural history) awakening to the fact that the "terra firma" on which we walk is in fact an array of seething, grinding tectonic plates (an example all too familiar to a native Californian). The difference, of course, is that while shifting tectonic plates seem to promise only devastation, in the form of violent earthquakes, the concept of a dynamic historical past holds the promise of intellectual growth.

REVISING OUR VIEW OF THE PAST

Rather than simply presenting an unchanging view of the past, historians instead are constantly searching for fresh sources, approaches, methodological tools, and interpretations in an effort to offer an ever-new past to the present. Or rather, a multitude of new pasts, since each historian's view of the past is at least slightly different from another's, sometimes dramatically different. In other words, a vigorous, many-sided debate among scholars is not only unavoidable but essential to the discipline. Even when differences are subtle, they can be important. When an interpretation entails a more sweeping challenge to an established way of interpreting a past event, process, or person, we call it revisionism.

Revisionism, together with less extensive shifts in approaches and interpretations, has been practiced since at least the time of the Greeks, as anyone who has examined the history of writing history is aware. Revisionism has, however, become particularly pronounced in the last few centuries, with the dramatic transformations in social, economic, and political life. As the pace of change quickens and its magnitude increases, there is a corresponding pressure to revise our presently held accounts of the past. This is because one of the most fundamental dimensions of our identity is provided by history, and as we change it too must change. When America was a simple agrarian society, without large cities, complex technology, and a vital world role to play, one kind of history sufficed. As the country grew, industrialized, and developed an array of perplexing social problems, new questions about the past had to be asked: What distinctive features were to be found on the frontier, and how had these affected national life and character? What was the historical experience of hitherto disempowered or exploited groups: African Americans, American Indians, Hispanics, Asians, or women? How did mass immigration impact upon politics, society, culture, and the economy? What were the historic patterns of relationship between social classes, and how were they changing? How was America's posture vis-à-vis the rest of the world being altered? These are only a few of the questions that have been posed by generations of historians since the late nineteenth century. Not surprisingly, a multiplicity of new approaches and interpretations have been offered in response, and previously neglected records and remnants of the past have become primary source material.

Americans did not initiate these new ways of looking at the past. Many European societies had begun to experience social and economic change much earlier, and this was reflected in their historical accounts.

The *philosophes* of the European Enlightenment developed a decidedly revisionist view of history and used it to great effect in their campaign against ignorance, superstition, and tyranny. Writers like Voltaire and Gibbon broke with long-established tendencies to write reverentially about states, rulers, and legal and ecclesiastical institutions. Their works, still rightly regarded as great classics in the writing of history, served as manifestoes in the eighteenth-century struggle to advance the cause of liberty and reason.

New Forms of Historical Consciousness

With the advent of the Industrial Revolution and attendant political unrest and demographic change at the end of the eighteenth century, some writers were moved to ask novel questions about the past. Thomas Malthus, that "gloomy" economist who began to point with alarm to the rapid and accelerating growth of population, complained that "the histories of mankind which we possess are, in general, histories only of the higher classes." He went on to suggest the composition of a history of the habits and mores of the general population based on accurate statistical information. Malthus was well aware of the massive intellectual labors that would have to be expended on such a project, but he nonetheless called upon future scholars to shoulder the burden:

> A satisfactory history of this kind, of one people and of one period, would require the constant and minute attention of many observing minds in local and general remarks on the state of the lower classes of society, and the causes that influenced it; and to draw accurate inferences upon this subject, a succession of such historians for some centuries would be necessary.[1]

Thus almost two hundred years ago Malthus outlined an agenda for the diligent historical demographers and social historians of our time whose labors are bearing rich fruit. Fortunately, the invention of the computer has significantly shortened the time he predicted would be required for such investigations.

The miseries thrust upon humanity by the early Industrial Revolution, coupled with the rise of a large, militant working class, led others to look for the historic roots of social conflict. Karl Marx is beyond question the most important of these commentators, and many historical studies have been immensely enriched by his powerful and trenchant analyses.

1 Thomas Malthus, *An Essay on Population* (London: J.M. Dent, 1952; first published 1798), 1: 16.

When he and Friedrich Engels issued the *Communist Manifesto* in 1848, it was intended as a clarion call to arms, not a work of scholarship. But the manifesto's assertion that the economic organization of society is the key to the past and that human history is driven by class struggle represents perhaps the most sweeping revisionist claim ever offered.

Marx's insistence that each historical epoch can be properly understood only by reference to its economic and material bases has profoundly altered the discipline of history. Virtually all subsequent historians, most of whom would object to being described as Marxists, are deeply in his debt. It is not a question of embracing Marxism as an ideology or accepting its critique of capitalism and vision of the future, elements that can be readily detached from the Marxist perspective on the past. The point is that Marx, like Malthus, forced people to question whether humanity is really well served by confining its historical attention to the doings of kings, statesmen, and generals—a questioning that admittedly had been initiated earlier by writers like Voltaire. It is by no means the case that political history, military history, or biography has withered on the vine as a result of these new perspectives. Indeed, some of the best work being done in those more traditional forms of history is the better for taking economic and social forces into account. Overall, the juxtaposition of the old forms with the new perspectives has created a complex, multifaceted debate—another manifestation of the vitality of history as process.

TOWARDS A "PEOPLE'S HISTORY"

I do not mean to suggest that without Malthus or Marx historians would have continued in their accustomed mold. Society was being transformed in too many ways for this to have been possible; the emergence of a variety of new approaches to historical inquiry was inevitable. One example is provided by a maverick English clergyman named John Richard Green, who wrote a very influential book published in 1874 entitled *A Short History of the English People*. In the preface to his work, Green declared:

> I have preferred to pass lightly and briefly over the details of foreign wars and diplomacies, the personal adventures of kings and nobles, the pomp of courts, or the intrigues of favourites, and to dwell at length on the incidents of that constitutional, intellectual, and social advance in which we read the history of the nation itself.[2]

2 John Richard Green, *A Short History of the English People* (New York: Harper and Brothers, 1899; first published 1874), xvii.

The striking inclusion in the title of Green's book was the word "People," and the author clearly believed that he was shifting the spotlight away from the historic elites to the mass of the population.

While many consider Green's *Short History of the English People* to be less innovative than he claimed, the book was enormously successful because the late nineteenth-century public thought it was breaking new ground in a way they considered necessary and important. It was reprinted sixteen times before the second edition appeared, posthumously, in 1887. Numerous pirated editions were published in the United States, and before the end of the century, Italian, French, German, Russian, and Chinese translations had appeared. Such an astonishing publishing success was due to something more than Green's literary gifts. Much of the world was then in the grip of vigorous populist and nationalist impulses, and the idea of a history of a people proved irresistibly attractive. It was a history, or rather a kind of history, whose time had come.

Needless to say, Green's *Short History* did not put an end to revisionism—no work ever has, or will. It might even be said to have intensified the ferment and accelerated the revisionist process. By making the "People" the centerpiece of historical inquiry, a number of essential questions were begged. Just who were the "People"? Were they the entire population, or some segment of it—workers or the middle class, perhaps? Was the focus to be on city dwellers or peasants? Should ethnic or religious minorities be taken into account? What about women—never a minority but hitherto ignored by historians—was their story to be considered? Furthermore, Green's focus on the *English people* implied that national entities were the appropriate units of historical investigation, yet there are many others, ranging from institutions to small communities, from regions to the entire world.

Minorities and Women Enter History

Revisionist efforts to recover and develop the history of minorities has necessarily often worked closely with political movements for the expansion of civil rights and the attainment of economic and social equality. Thus in the early decades of this century the great African-American historian W. E. B. DuBois was a major figure in the struggle for racial equality. His own writings, along with his participation in the founding of the *Journal of Negro History,* enhanced the visibility of African Americans and helped rescue their history from the patronizing or frankly racist attitudes of most white historians of the period. An expansion of interest in black history during the last several decades obviously is linked to the intensification of the struggle for civic, social, and economic equality. In revealing the historic patterns of race relations, this new body of scholarship has served to enhance the pride and clarify the goals of African Americans. Moreover, it has educated other Americans about the nature and consequences of racism, thereby fostering progress towards a society of greater justice and opportunity. Much the same can be said of the burgeoning scholarship on the history of Hispanics, American Indians, and other ethnic minorities.

Women's history has been particularly active during the last few decades, and, like the history of ethnic minorities, it can be correlated to vigorous political and social movements. Since historical invisibility is a virtually universal corollary to powerlessness, the campaign to establish gender equality necessarily required a historical component. Just as the "People" in the title of Green's *Short History* served as a rallying cry for populist and national groups many years ago, June Sochen's *Herstory* (1974) did the same for the women's movement. Although many important works in women's history had appeared before, *Herstory*, the title of this volume, evoked in a single word the necessity for a story very different from those that had been told for so long by male historians.[3]

It should not be imagined that histories of minorities or women are designed or undertaken merely to serve as appendages to political causes. The same demanding criteria regarding the evaluation of sources, the marshalling of evidence, and the deployment of literary skill are used in assessing these histories as in any other. It is a blend of diligence, skepticism, imagination, judiciousness, and humor that pays big dividends to historians in any field. Nor should these newer bodies of scholarship be seen as representing some sort of ethnic- or gender-related orthodoxy. None is any more monolithic than any other field of history. Indeed, some of the most vigorous and interesting debates within the profession occur in these newer, albeit politically charged, areas.

One important point of disagreement within minority history involves the same concern manifested in the nineteenth century over whether to focus on an elite group or all of the population. Many of the earlier studies tended to concentrate on the achievements of extraordinary persons. Critics have charged that, whatever the merits of these works in producing positive role models, they often serve to obscure the historical realities of the lives of the masses of the disempowered. As a result, there

3 June Sochen, *Herstory: A Woman's View of American History* (New York: Alfred Publishing Co., 1974).

has been a shift in women's and minority history towards incorporating some of the methods and approaches of social history. This particular application of "history from below" exemplifies not only revisionism but also the process of cross-fertilization among various fields of history. Furthermore, while women's history continues to exist as an important field, there has been a broadening from its base into "gender studies," a field devoted to investigating the ways in which gender identities, both overt and latent, have shaped all aspects of the human experience.

So far, the examples of historical scholarship we have examined, while exhibiting the concept of history as process, can be fitted into the "history as story" format. That is, most of them have a narrative structure in which a sequence of connected events occurring within a span of time is rendered by the historian to create pattern and meaning. Even when large social aggregates like classes or ethnic groups rather than individuals are the centerpiece of the story, they can still usually be made to function as (individualized) characters in a complex story. Marx's scheme of history is a good example, with (at one stage) its rising bourgeoisie deployed against a crumbling feudal nobility. The unfolding of the Marxist story of class conflict is marked by such significant events or movements as the rapid growth of towns, the Protestant Reformation, the invention of the steam engine, the French Revolution, and the "scramble for Africa" by colony-hungry European powers in the late nineteenth century. But the twentieth century has witnessed the emergence of varieties of history that largely abandon the investigation of change over time. We will briefly examine two of them: the Annales school and cliometrics.

THE ANNALES SCHOOL AND CLIOMETRICS

A historical journal established in France in 1929 provided the forum for a new kind of historical scholarship, one that aimed at nothing less than recapturing the totality of human experience. By employing the methods and techniques of the social sciences, the scholars connected to this new enterprise sought to delineate all aspects of past societies, with an emphasis on those enduring patterns of culture that changed slowly if at all. The journal of this new school of historians was called *Annales d'histoire économique et sociale*; hence practitioners of this kind of history came to be called Annalistes. Central to the Annalistes' approach was a disparagement of event-oriented history. Those innumerable events that historians had charged with significance and arranged in various configurations to produce narrative accounts were regarded by the Annalistes as mere surface ripples on the ocean of society. In the new school, the traditional concern with events was replaced by a search for society's *mentalités*, the ways of life and the values that persisted despite major political and social upheavals.

One of the foremost Annalistes was Fernand Braudel, whose magisterial study *The Mediterranean and the Mediterranean World in the Age of Philip II* appeared in 1949. Braudel's revisionism involved not only an emphasis on persistent patterns of life but also the use of the Mediterranean basin as the setting for his analysis, as opposed to some political entity like Spain or France. A favorite phrase of Braudel and other Annalistes was the *longue durée*, a vast sweep of time during which little change occurred. Regarding the difficulty in gaining acceptance for this new and radically different perspective in the historical profession, Braudel commented:

> For the historian, accepting the *longue durée* entails a readiness to change his style, his attitudes, a whole reversal in his thinking, a whole new way of conceiving social affairs. It means becoming used to a slower tempo, which sometimes almost borders on the motionless.[4]

Although Braudel himself by no means neglected "events" altogether, it is clear that the Annaliste approach in its purest form tends virtually to preclude any sense of history as story.

A close partnership between historians and other social scientists is an important tenet of the Annales school. The attempt to delineate cultural patterns with little attention to change over time is an approach similar to that employed by many anthropologists and sociologists. An even newer field of history called cliometrics, after Clio (pronounced CLY-oh) the Greek muse of history, evinces a similar determination to utilize social science methodologies. Cliometricians are those scholars who employ quantification to reveal historical pattern and meaning. Obviously something a good deal more is requisite than an ability or willingness to count, which historians have been doing since Herodotus (the ancient Greek historian). Cliometricians use computers, sophisticated programs, and social science models in their analyses. They also tend to disparage source material that cannot be quantified, so many of the records relied upon by other historians in fashioning their accounts are devalued as "soft" or "impressionistic" evidence, to be used only reluctantly and in strict subordination to the numeric data. Clearly, only those areas of historical study for which there

4 Fernand Braudel, *On History*, translated by Sarah Matthews (Chicago: University of Chicago Press, 1980), 33.

is an ample supply of records yielding quantifiable data are amenable to such an approach. For this reason, economic history has been a particularly active area of cliometric investigation—and a particularly controversial one.

Among the most controversial of the cliometric studies is Robert Fogel's and Stanley Engerman's ringingly revisionist book, *Time on the Cross* (1974), a study of slavery in the United States. Deploying a formidable array of charts, graphs, and statistics, the authors set out to disprove a number of time-honored beliefs about slavery, such as its alleged inefficiency compared to a free economy. The picture of American slavery in *Time on the Cross* is that of a thriving, expanding institution in both its agricultural and industrial components. Besides promoting their own revisionist view of slavery, Fogel and Engerman made sweeping claims about the ability of cliometrics to transform economic history across a broad front:

> The cliometricians have downgraded the role of technological change in American economic advance; they have controverted the claim that railroads were necessary to the settlement and exploitation of the West; they have contended that the boom and bust of the 1830s and early 1840s were the consequences of developments in Mexico and Britain rather than the policies of Andrew Jackson; and they have rejected the contention that the Civil War greatly accelerated the industrialization of the nation.[5]

Despite this assertion, none of these new interpretations has gone unchallenged. Indeed, their work helped trigger a major counterattack across a broad front, not only against some of the cliometricians' interpretations but against much of their methodology as well. Perhaps the most vigorous assault came from Jacques Barzun, whose *Clio and the Doctors* appeared in the same year as Fogel's and Engerman's study. Barzun made an eloquent plea for keeping history within the tradition of humane letters, resisting the temptation to use the latest piece of technology or scientific model. And, as the subtitle of his book indicates, Barzun was writing not only about the cliometricians but about another new group, the psychohistorians, as well.[6]

5 Robert Fogel and Stanley L. Engerman, *Time on the Cross: The Economics of American Negro Slavery* (Boston and Toronto: Little, Brown, & Co., 1974), 1: 7.
6 Jacques Barzun, *Clio and the Doctors: Psycho-History, Quanto-History, and History* (Chicago: University of Chicago Press, 1974).

PSYCHOLOGY AND HISTORY

Psychohistory represents an attempt to apply to historical study the methods and insights developed by Sigmund Freud and other psychological theorists during the past hundred years or so. In dealing with the question of motives, historians often have to look beneath the surface in an effort to discern the real as distinct from the alleged reason for an action or policy. Generally they recognize that to move beyond the manifest content of the sources tends to render such judgments tentative and problematic. Psychohistorians, however, are less disposed to be tentative when it comes to making assumptions. Bolstered by a belief in the scientific soundness of clinical evidence, psychohistory undertakes to expose what is claimed to be the real but hitherto hidden face of the past. One of the leading practitioners of psychobiography, the late Fawn Brodie, described in her revisionist study of Thomas Jefferson the nature of the psychohistorical approach as well as the barriers to its acceptance:

> The idea that a man's inner life affects every aspect of his intellectual life and also his decision-making should need no defense today. To illuminate this relationship, however, requires certain biographical techniques that make some historians uncomfortable. One must look for feeling as well as fact, for nuance and metaphor as well as idea and action.[7]

One important distinction between psychohistory and some of the other newer approaches to history that draw upon social science methodology is that psychohistory is altogether compatible with history as story. Indeed, it has assisted in the revival of biography, a traditional genre generally disparaged by the Annalistes and others concerned with broad, enduring patterns of social life and culture. In some respects, psychobiography and the Annales school are opposite poles; it is hard to imagine points of focus more different than the life of an individual on the one hand and the mentalité of an entire civilization during a vast sweep of time on the other. Of course, psychohistorians are not necessarily biographers. The methods and insights of social psychology can provide many other dimensions to the study of social history: the phenomenon of crowd psychology during times of political or social turbulence, for example. They can prove useful to Annalistes as well, provided that the mass psychological patterns being examined are of an enduring nature.

---

7 Fawn Brodie, *Thomas Jefferson: An Intimate History* (New York: Norton, 1974), 16.

Microhistory and Macrohistory

In recent decades there has been an interest by some historical scholars in very tightly focused studies of single small communities, while others have written histories from a global perspective. A leading example of the former is the French historian Emmanuel Le Roy Ladurie's study of the medieval French village of Montaillou over a thirty-year period.[8] The chance survival of Inquisition records for this village allowed the author to plumb the depths of the local peasants' views on such matters as childhood, marriage, magic, religion, and the afterlife—a kind of Annaliste approach with an extremely local focus. As for global history, although there were important early precursors such as the great North African scholar Ibn Khaldun (1332–1406), the pioneering figure in the twentieth century was the British scholar Arnold J. Toynbee. His twelve-volume *A Study of History*,[9] with its vast sweeps of time and comparisons of major civilizations, inspired others to broaden their approach far beyond the confines of the nation state or even a particular culture. An especially avid disciple of Toynbee was the American historian William H. McNeill, whose numerous studies of this type[10] have had an enormous impact on historical writing. With rapidly increasing globalization, this kind of historical scholarship is certain to expand further.

Postmodernism

The last few decades have seen the rise of a cluster of methodologies that go under the name "postmodernism." Originating in European, and especially French literary theory, this approach represents what some have called the "linguistic turn" in historical studies. Some of the key formulators of the body of theory on which postmodernism is based are Michel Foucault, Jacques Derrida, and Jacques Lacan.

A method known as "deconstructionism" lies at the heart of postmodernist analysis of many forms of art and literature, as well as historical literature. Essentially, a historical deconstuctionist analysis explores the operation of key "texts" and "discourses" around which societies are organized. These texts and discourses, which are largely constructed to bolster

8 Emmanuel Le Roy Ladurie, *Montaillou: The Promised Land of Error*, trans. Barbara Bray (New York: George Braziller, 1978). The book was first published in French in 1975.
9 Arnold J. Toynbee, *A Study of History*, 12 vols. (London: Oxford University Press, 1948–61).
10 See, for example, William H. McNeill, *The Global Condition: Conquerors, Catastrophes, and Community* (Princeton: Princeton University Press, 1992).

the power of social elites and dominant ideologies, can range from formal political or constitutional documents through works of literature to all forms of social commentary and popular entertainment. Such "discourses," unrecognized as such by the vast majority of the society being studied, can include nonlingual sources as well, such as architecture, film, and all kinds of images. Deconstructionists endeavor to strip away the positive or idealistic facades of dominant discourses and to show them for what they are: tools for legitimating political, social, economic, and cultural oppression. This approach is called postmodernist in part because it challenges the essentially modern belief (dominant since the Enlightenment) that human institutions, guided by reason and science, have tended to become progressively more tolerant and humane.

In the United States, postmodernism was brought forcefully to the attention of most historians in the late 1970s by the translation into English of Michel Foucault's *Discipline and Punish*,[11] a book first published in France in 1975. This impressive, though still controversial, postmodernist analysis is concerned with the evolution of the idea of the modern prison in the eighteenth and nineteenth centuries. Whereas previous historians had tended to see marked progress in the treatment of criminals (e.g. the end of barbaric forms of execution, new standards of decency in prisons, the concept of rehabilitation), Foucault depicted the new rehabilatory regimen instituted in prisons as far more intrusive than the old system, as well as being destructive of the individual and totalitarian in its implications. Indeed Foucault tended to see the prison as almost a microcosm of modern society, whose increasingly powerful and sophisticated devices for marginalizing and suppressing deviant behavior are part of a relentless drive to produce a single acceptable human type: rational, docile, and materialistic.

Like the idea of the modern prison, there are few elements of any society that cannot be "deconstructed" to reveal the manner in which they bolster the power of elites, maintain hierarchical distinctions, and marginalize those who are seen as different. Postmodernism, which is prominent today in the field of cultural history, has had a particularly marked effect on women's history, gender studies, and the history of imperialism, and it is still controversial. Critics claim that its emphasis on oppression and marginalization is a distortion of the past, and that it too readily lends itself to present-day polemical purposes and political causes, to the detriment of scholarly rigor. Another concern is that postmodernism's

11 Michel Foucault, *Discipline and Punish: The Birth of the Prison*, trans. Alan Sheridan (Harmondswoth: Penguin Books, 1979).

emphasis on the slipperiness and infinite malleability of language, together with its denial of the possibility of objectivity in our understanding of human affairs, amounts to a kind of philosophical nihilism.[12] Some of the more ideologically driven works in this genre do indeed bear out these concerns. However, a postmodernist approach, when used sensitively, selectively, and with sufficient detachment from ideological commitments and identity politics, can be a helpful tool in studying history.

A Multitude of Avenues to the Past

The foregoing examples of changes in the way historians have approached the past during the last couple of centuries were introduced in an attempt to illustrate the concept of history as a dynamic process. While the above is only a cursory survey at best, clearly, "history as story" is not a dead form. In spite of the appearance of new kinds of analysis, it seems likely that the narrative mode of writing history is still dominant. What is crucial to grasp is that there is an enormous variety of narrative approaches and that new ones will continue to appear. There is, quite simply, no such thing as a "definitive" treatment of any topic. Although this term is sometimes applied to a particularly impressive work of scholarship, its application would, if taken literally, foreclose all subsequent inquiry on a given topic. Then history would indeed evolve into that static body of knowledge so often imagined by those with too little exposure to it as a discipline.

Historiography, which in its broadest sense means the history of history writing, is a demanding and vitally important branch of the discipline of history. Students who have not taken a course in historiography before embarking upon advanced undergraduate research projects would be well-advised to read some of the general works on the subject.[13] It is important to have some notion of historiography in this broad sense before turning to our discussion of bibliographic research on a given topic. Once you are engaged in research for a project, the term historiography will be encountered in its narrower meaning: the various ways scholars have approached and interpreted the subject(s) you have chosen to investigate. Every topic has its own historiography, and an understanding of its dimensions is essential, not only for constructing a historiographic essay,

12 S. Joyce Appleby, Lynn Hunt, and Margaret Jacob, *Telling the Truth about History* (New York and London: W. W. Norton & Co., 1995), especially 198–237.
13 See, for example, Ernst Breisach, *Historiography, Ancient, Medieval, and Modern,* 2d ed. (Chicago: University of Chicago Press, 1994).

but also for writing a research paper using primary sources. These are the two types of historical writing that will be explored in later chapters. Before undertaking the writing of either a historiographic essay or a research paper, however, it is necessary to know the different types of historical sources and how to find them, matters the next two chapters will explore.

CHAPTER TWO

The Nature and Variety of Historical Sources

As we saw in Chapter One, history is an intellectual discipline marked by ongoing change, punctuated by the periodic appearance of major revisionist works. Historians are constantly reviewing and rethinking the past, discovering new patterns and meanings. In this process, they depend upon the tangible remains of the past for source materials. Any remnant of the past can serve the purpose. Although written records tend to predominate as source materials in most fields of history, in others (particularly ancient and medieval) there is often a heavy reliance on artifacts. Such materials are of importance to those studying modern history as well. Weapons, coins, household utensils, cathedrals, statues, and films can cast as much light on the past as diaries, letters, and newspapers. Whether these historical raw materials are written records or artifacts we refer to them as primary sources. The written histories that historians fashion from these (primary) sources in turn become (secondary) sources for subsequent investigators.

PRIMARY SOURCES

Written primary sources can be divided into two major categories: manuscript sources and published sources. For historians, a manuscript is any handwritten or typewritten record or communication that has not been printed or otherwise duplicated in significant quantities for public dissemination. It can be anything from a laundry list to the minutes of a cabinet meeting in the Oval Office. Usually manuscript materials were intended for private or at least restricted use, although something like the notes for a speech that was never delivered also would be considered a manuscript source. A manuscript can be as intensely personal as a diary or as institutional as a roster of Egyptian temple scribes. There is virtually no kind of written record that has not been used, or might some day be used, as a primary source. As social history and other new approaches to the past evolve, even the seemingly most trivial or mundane remnants may acquire significance.

Manuscript Sources

Most of our attention will be devoted to published primary sources, since undergraduate researchers in university libraries usually have only limited access to manuscript source materials. But in many cases, there may be significant manuscript collections close at hand. Perhaps your university library has a special collections or manuscript department containing important materials. There also may be nearby community libraries, local historical societies, or private individuals with such resources. A look through any of these collections might prove extremely rewarding, depending on your subject. If you are researching a topic of local history, you are more likely to be afforded the opportunity to get your hands on manuscript materials. In any event, it is worthwhile to investigate the availability of manuscript collections in your locality; this may even help you choose a viable research topic, though it should be realized that access to many major manuscript collections is limited to professional historians and advanced graduate students.

Published Sources

Published primary sources can be divided into two categories: 1) Manuscript materials such as letters, diaries, and memoranda, usually intended as private, sometimes intimate documents, often published after the death of their authors; 2) Materials that were intended from the outset to be printed and made public—for example newspaper articles, congressional debates, autobiographies, annual company reports, and reports of the United States Census.

There are few major political figures in the modern world, particularly the United States, whose writings have not been published. Library shelves groan with the massive collected works of our presidents and major public figures. Historical leaders of other societies are also well represented, so that when researching the activities of the wielders of power or shapers of opinion you will usually find no shortage of published primary sources. While many of these writings were not, strictly speaking, intended for public consumption, it is scarcely surprising that they eventually appear in published form. Those attaining high office during the last couple of centuries could hardly expect that their papers would remain confidential for very long after their deaths. Indeed, the measure of immortality attainable through the posthumous publication of one's collected papers is apt to be a component of political ambition. Some leaders might be considered as "playing to posterity," at least part of the time; for this reason, their papers must therefore be read and considered with an additional measure of critical judgment.

The injunction to be critical of the papers of society's leaders applies with special force to personal memoirs and autobiographies written "after the fact," when these author/subjects were at the end of their careers or in retirement. These types of published sources require interpretive care on two grounds. First, it must be remembered that the validity of such sources depends to a considerable extent on the author's ability to recall events that may have occurred much earlier in his or her life. Obviously there must always be a presumed erosion of reliability in such recollections, one that increases with the amount of time that has elapsed. As the historian Arthur M. Schlesinger Jr. observes in the preface to his own recently published autobiography: "The generic title for all memoirs should be *Things I Remember . . . and Things I Think I Remember.*"[1] Second, autobiographies and memoirs are usually self-serving, or at least should be assumed to be so. As mentioned, in creating these accounts, politicians and other public leaders may have been anxious to secure their place in history. Certain episodes in their lives may therefore be given more prominence than they deserve as well as a highly favorable interpretation, while others, which may be less flattering, may be slighted, distorted, or ignored altogether. The same applies to the descriptions of the various other persons who are discussed in these accounts. This by no means renders memoirs or autobiographies worthless as source materials. Among other things, they provide invaluable insights into the personalities of leading figures. As with all source materials, however, the historian must begin by asking the purpose for which they were written or published, and then proceed with an appropriate measure of caution and skepticism.

A skeptical approach is also in order when considering materials like the published letters and diaries of public figures. These sources are perhaps more trustworthy in one respect, since they are contemporary with the events and not therefore subject to the corrosive effects of time on memory. Even in this case, however, we must consider the author's

---

1 Arthur M. Schlesinger Jr., *A Life in the Twentieth Century: Innocent Beginnings, 1917–1950* (Boston: Houghton Mifflin, 2000), xiii.

motives, ignorance, or capacity for self-deception. Moreover, published source materials are frequently only a selection, and sometimes quite a small one, of the total body of the person's writings. We must therefore take into account the built-in bias of the selecting or editing process. How representative of the whole are the documents that are published? Did a favorably disposed editor (perhaps a member of the family) suppress un-flattering material? Even the most professional and even-handed editor must make painful choices about what materials to leave out. This is why historians always consult the largest and best-edited collection of primary sources available, assuming of course that they do not have access to manuscript sources.

Somewhat different considerations apply to those written primary sources particularly valued by social historians. The development of inter-est in "history from below" has encouraged the finding and publication of the writings of ordinary people who, presumably, never dreamed their words would be published. The chance survival and later publication of the diary of an American pioneer woman or the letters of a soldier in the Crimean War can vividly illuminate the lives and experiences of ordinary people. This does not mean, of course, that such writings can be accepted uncritically. While the authors of such documents were no doubt bliss-fully unconcerned about the opinion of posterity, their writing, too, can be expected to reflect the normal human biases and blind spots. These "shortcomings" need not necessarily get in the way of our understanding; they may indeed be precisely the sort of thing for which we are looking.

Let us now turn to primary source materials like newspapers, maga-zines, and official reports of government or private institutions. Not only were these intended from the outset to be made public, in many cases they were designed to influence public opinion. This is certainly the case with newspapers, whose editorial policies must usually be taken into ac-count. Thus to accept a newspaper account of one of the Lincoln-Dou-glas debates without considering the paper's political orientation would be a major critical lapse. Even if an article displayed no detectable bias, we would have to consider the problems inherent in relying upon a single reporter's account of the event: his vantage point, his ability to hear all that was said from the podium, the reactions of those in the crowd that were closest to him, and so on. Diligent historians assemble as many such accounts as they can, treating each of them critically, sorting out obvious biases and errors, and fashioning as accurate a reconstruction as possible.

Other examples of print media must be approached in much the same way. Magazines, journals, and pamphlets all offer a vast storehouse of facts and prejudices. Like newspapers, they can reveal a great deal that the authors and editors never intended. Popular literature, sheet music, sermons, and plays also can tell us much about a society's common, unexamined assumptions. Consider the value of sources like this for, say, investigating nineteenth-century American attitudes toward gender roles or racial stereotyping. However, it is necessary to read such material in two quite different ways. On the one hand, the historian must try to see the work as contemporaries did, an approach that requires both knowledge of the time and empathy for its people. Simultaneously, the material must be viewed through the critical, dispassionate eyes of a modern scholar who is posing questions that nineteenth-century people could not or did not ask.

There is an enormous variety and range of primary sources, only a few of which have been touched upon here. When undertaking a research paper on a particular topic, it is well worth your time to first consider all the types of sources that might be used. A little investigation and imagination may make it possible for you to use different kinds of sources than those employed by any previous scholars who have researched your same topic. Or it may enable you to approach the sources from a whole new perspective. Conversely, if you are in the midst of trying to decide upon a good topic, an awareness of the range of sources available to you might point you towards a highly interesting topic that you otherwise might not have considered.

Secondary Works

Secondary works or sources come in a great variety as well—from multivolume works of collective scholarship to short essays, and from general histories to the most specialized monographs. Next we will consider some of the different forms written histories can take: books, essays, and articles.

Books
Books are such a universal and commonplace feature of academic life that students seldom ponder their diversity or unique structures. We can begin our consideration of the diversity of the types of history books with the breadth or narrowness of the subject. The extremes would be a textbook on the history of the world from the advent of human life to the present, and a study of a single individual or small community over a short span of time. In between these extremes are histories of such entities as civiliza-

tions, regions, nation-states, or social classes. Moreover, the approach can be political, social, economic, cultural, or some combination of these. Furthermore, its style can be narrative or analytical. The focus can be on individuals or social aggregates. The tone and style may be "popular" or "scholarly"—that is, it may be calculated to appeal to a wide, nonprofessional readership, or it may bristle with footnotes, statistics, and closely reasoned analysis designed for the author's scholarly peers.

Another method of distinguishing between history books is whether they are based chiefly on primary or secondary sources. As a rule, the broader the topic, the more the author relies on secondary works. Thus a book entitled *A History of the World* (or even *A History of the United States*) will probably not have many primary sources in its bibliography. You can see this for yourself by examining the bibliographies of one of the textbooks you have used (or are using) in a history survey course. Notice that the author's or authors' (many textbooks have multiple authors) account is fashioned out of the more specialized studies of other historians. New editions of texts are issued not only to bring the story up to the present, but to revise in light of the most recent specialized scholarship. In this way the fruits of the latest scholarship enter the general survey texts and hence the classroom.

Survey textbooks and other general accounts are sometimes referred to as works of synthesis, because they synthesize or bring together the more specialized works of others. Those more specialized works, especially when fairly narrow in scope and based on primary sources, are called monographs. Some monographs are simply detailed narrative accounts of particular subjects, but others attempt to break fresh interpretive ground and are thus important vehicles for historical revisionism. This does not mean, however, that works of synthesis cannot offer revisionist interpretations, for many of the most important revisionist works are those that offer fresh ways of interpreting the recent secondary literature. Also, this discussion of monographs and works of synthesis might imply a sharper barrier between them than in fact exists. Many history books, having elements of both types, cannot be so tidily classified. Furthermore, the author of even the narrowest monograph is expected to take fully into account the other specialized scholarship on the topic, that is, to place his or her analysis within a historiographic frame of reference.

The historian's craft is both an individual and a collective enterprise. It is a fact that historians need and depend upon the contributions of other scholars, and it is also true that many works of history are jointly written. In some cases two or more scholars may work closely together in both the research and writing. More commonly a general editor will coordinate the efforts of a team of historians, each of whom is given primary responsibility for a portion of the whole. A couple of examples are *The Oxford History of England* and *The Cambridge History of Islam*, both of them sponsored by large university presses. Other "joint" projects are published under the auspices of organizations like the United Nations, such as the UNESCO-sponsored *General History of Africa*. Collective authorship can be an effective means of bringing to bear a degree of expertise that would not be attainable if such vast projects were undertaken by a single author. There is also a significant saving of time involved, though large joint projects have their own pitfalls, delays, and frustrations that sorely test the skill and patience of general editors.

Whether scholarly monographs or survey texts, all history books have structural similarities that are important to note, especially when you are trying to determine quickly the approach, interpretation, and scope of a particular volume. The proper approach to your reading will be taken up in more detail in Chapter Four, but a few pointers are in order here. A book's title will usually be descriptive of its scope, but the subtitle (if there is one) will often tell you more. Recall the psychobiography of Jefferson by Fawn Brodie discussed in Chapter One. The title itself, *Thomas Jefferson*, indicates nothing more than that it is a biography. But the subtitle, *An Intimate History*, gives you a strong clue that this is not a standard political biography of Jefferson the public figure. By looking at the chapter headings in the book's table of contents and reading the introduction, the approach and scope of the work should become clear. Also, a look at the index will let you preview a book quickly for desired information.

Essays

An essay (sometimes simply called a "chapter") is a short, self-contained study, usually bound with similar works in book form. An essay can be narrow or broad in scope, based on primary or secondary sources, and chiefly narrative or assertively interpretive. It is a versatile, effective literary form for historians, as it is for scholars in the other humanities. Usually, essays by different authors writing on different aspects of the same general topic or field are combined into a single work with a title such as Essays in Business History. The range of essays in such a volume might be very wide, for example from an analysis of merchant enterprise in fourteenth-century Florence to a study of the start-up of high-tech industries in California.

Sometimes the essays will have been published previously, perhaps in a different form such as an article in a scholarly journal. Often the earlier articles and essays of eminent historians will be gathered together and published. Sometimes each member of a group of historians who were trained by or highly admire the same scholar will contribute an essay to a book published in the mentor's honor, sometimes on the occasion of that person's retirement. Such a collection is called a *Festschrift*, a German word meaning a presentation volume of essays dedicated to someone.[2]

Articles

Similar to essays in structure, length, and purpose, scholarly articles are an even more important segment of the body of secondary works. They are published in scholarly periodicals, or journals, of which there is an enormous variety. Articles are often the format in which historians launch new interpretations. The process of revisionism would be greatly retarded if scholarly journals were not able to publish and disseminate historical findings. For you, the student researcher, to ignore articles and confine your attention to the available books would be to miss much of the freshest and most provocative literature on your subject. An appreciation of this large, diverse body of scholarship requires some understanding of the journals themselves, which, in turn, will lead us to a consideration of the structure of the historical profession itself.

Usually, a periodical publication in which scholarly articles are published is called a journal. The term "magazine" should, for the most part, be confined to those periodicals of a more popular bent such as *Newsweek* or the *Atlantic Monthly*. There are a few historical periodicals, like the British publication *History Today,* that have a popular magazine format, with short, amply illustrated articles designed to appeal to a wider readership. For the most part, however, historical journals are designed for a professional readership and feature lengthy, detailed articles, some of which can be daunting to the nonspecialist. But this should not intimidate the undergraduate researcher; a history student who is properly launched on a particular topic should find most of the scholarly articles on his or her topic both readable and stimulating.

Many historical journals are published by associations of historians, with the costs of publication defrayed in part by membership subscriptions. In the United States, one of the leading historical journals is the

2 An example is *Ideas and Institutions of Victorian Britain. Essays in Honour of George Kitson Clark,* ed. Robert Robson (London: Bell & Sons, 1967). The title of this book gives no clue to the specialized essays it contains. For this reason, essays are sometimes called the "hidden literature." How to find this "hidden literature" will be one of our concerns in the next chapter.

American Historical Review, the official organ of the American Historical Association (AHA). The AHA is the major "umbrella" organization for historians in the country; its thousands of members include historians of almost every conceivable specialization or field of interest. Accordingly, the *American Historical Review* does not specialize in any one historical field. In each of its five annual issues, there might be articles on such diverse topics as modern Europe, Tang Dynasty China, Hellenistic Egypt, and colonial America. Methodologically, the many articles represent all approaches to the past. Similarly, the hundreds of pages of book reviews that appear in each issue of this journal cover titles in all fields of history. Book reviews play a vitally important role in the evaluation and analysis of historical works. They are part of the elaborate apparatus by which new views in history are subjected to close critical scrutiny.

The *American Historical Review* is notable not just for its size and importance, but also because it is atypical of historical journals, the great majority of which have some kind of special focus. For example, The *Journal of American History* is published by the Organization of American Historians (OAH), whose members' primary interest is the history of the United States. This journal, as its name suggests, publishes articles and book reviews in the field of American history. The scope of many other journals is defined by their titles, e.g. *The Journal of Modern History, The Journal of African Studies, The Journal of Contemporary History,* and *Byzantine Studies.* Some specialize not in time periods or geographic areas, but on methodological approaches, such as *The Journal of Social History* and *The International Journal of Psychohistory.* Most are produced under the auspices of some professional organization. The North American Conference on British Studies, for example, supports the publication of two, *Albion* and *The Journal of British Studies.*

Many have a narrow focus. Journals of local history are a prime example, and there is a great abundance of such publications in the United States. State historical societies and many societies devoted to the history of cities and other localities publish their own journals, which researchers ignore at their peril. Many important revisionist interpretations are produced in the form of article-length studies in local history journals.

Local studies are not only important in and of themselves, but they also offer a valuable means of validating or refuting general historical hypotheses. Any assertion about a society's characteristics can be tested by examining particular localities in great detail. How, for example, would you attempt to test the claim that there was a high degree of social mobility in nineteenth-century America? Since searching for an answer to this question involves data that must be tracked over successive generations, the analysis of massive amounts of occupational data from the U.S. Census as well as plenty of other material, a local study is often the most feasible procedure. One town's records would be much easier to decipher than those of the nation. Obviously, no single study of any single town could sustain or overturn the general hypothesis, but a number of investigations might. Local studies, therefore, can and do contribute to an ever-emerging picture of regional or national history. Sometimes, they serve the important purpose of pointing out significant differences among states, regions, or localities.

Dissertations and Conference Papers

Turning from those secondary sources readily accessible in published form, such as books, essays, and articles, let us consider two other forms in which new findings are presented, scholarly dissertations and conference papers. A Doctorate of Philosophy (Ph.D.) is the highest academic degree in history, and its completion requires the writing of a scholarly dissertation, usually on a rather narrow topic and based on intensive research in primary sources. The granting of a Ph.D. in history follows the certifying by a committee of historians that the candidate's dissertation meets the standards of the profession. A dissertation is expected to demonstrate its author's critical acumen, writing abilities, and knowledge of the relevant primary and secondary sources. Dissertations are also usually expected to offer original analyses and interpretations. They can therefore be important works of new scholarship, and even of revisionist interpretation. Some are published subsequently as books. Others will be substantially revised before ultimately being published or will eventually appear, after some modification, as journal articles. Even in their unrevised form, recent dissertations can be important tools for researchers. Not only do they offer new interpretations, but their bibliographies are apt to be especially complete and are therefore excellent guides to the topic's sources.[3]

Conference papers, delivered by historians to their peers at scholarly conferences (often the meetings of organizations like the AHA), might be described as the "cutting edge" of new scholarship. In many cases, this is the initial form in which the results of a historian's findings are made public and subjected to scrutiny and criticism. Often on the basis of the criti-

3 A bound copy of each dissertation is available in the library of the university granting the Ph.D., and often an extra copy is available through the interlibrary loan system. For those wishing to acquire their own copy, dissertations are available on microfilm and can be purchased from University Microfilms Corporation.

cism received at a conference, a historian will revise his or her work before submitting it for publication. Typically, a conference paper will be presented as part of a panel discussion that will hear and consider two or three papers on similar topics. After an introduction by the scholar chairing the panel, each presenter will read his or her work. After the papers have been read aloud (each requiring twenty minutes or so), a commentary on the papers is given by a scholarly expert (in the field) on the panel. Sometimes printed versions of the papers are made available to prospective members of the audience beforehand, so they come to the session already familiar with the presenter's arguments. After all the papers have been read, the commentator offers criticism, advice, and often the delineation of some themes or threads that tie the papers together. At this point the audience is free to question, challenge, help refine, or offer counterinterpretations to points made in the papers. This can be a highly stimulating, sometimes acrimonious exchange, but it is one of the principal means by which new views are expressed and modified prior to publication.

To get some idea of how this process operates, let us consider the largest historical conference of them all: the annual meeting of the AHA. Held over a four-day period, the AHA's annual meeting is a vast smorgasbord of offerings, with clusters of panels running simultaneously. At the January 2001 meeting in Boston, for example, there were no fewer than 160 panels on everything from "Narrating Salem Witchcraft as an Episode in Frontier History" to "Terror and Population Politics under Nazi and Soviet Power: Comparative Explorations."[4] Each of the panels tends to attract for its audience specialists in the particular field, though many participants find it stimulating to attend at least a few panels well outside their primary areas of interest.

In addition to the panels, the annual meeting is an occasion for publishers of scholarly books in history to display their wares. This is an important source of information for historians about the latest publications in the field. There are also numerous opportunities for social and intellectual exchanges during conferences: individual encounters, receptions, and the luncheons of the many historical societies affiliated to the AHA. It is these affiliated societies (subgroups of the AHA's membership) that are apt to be the primary focus of most historians' professional involvement. Many if not most of these smaller groups also hold their own regular meetings and conferences independently of the AHA meeting. Like the

4 American Historical Association, *Program of the 115th Annual Meeting*, January 4–7, 2001. (Washington, D.C.: American Historical Association, 2000).

specialized journals that cater to particular fields, the hundreds of historical societies are organized along geographic, cultural, chronological, or methodological bases. Such groups as the Medieval Academy of America, the American Conference on Irish Studies, the Society for the History of Technology, and the World History Society represent crucial parts of the infrastructure of the historical profession.

This account of the basic organizational features of the profession is introduced in order to give some sense of the dynamic and cooperative character of modern scholarship. It is important for you to realize that most books and articles you will encounter were not written by "ivory tower" types working in complete isolation, but by men and women developing and refining their views in relation to the methods and criticisms of others. This is what we mean when we describe the historical profession, or some segment of it, as a "community of scholars."

But now it is time to go the sources. In the next chapter we will explore the various methods of finding the works you will need to research your topic.

CHAPTER THREE

Finding Your Sources: The Library Catalog and Beyond

A child who asks for an item of general information will often be told to "look it up." This response, though it may sometimes stem from an unwillingness to admit ignorance, is an educationally sound one. Its tendency is to make the child a self-directed learner and to develop basic research skills. A children's encyclopedia or a "book of knowledge" may be the extent of the materials available in the home, but the lesson imparted is invaluable: that a storehouse of accumulated information is literally at one's fingertips. Beyond the home, the maturing student discovers the richer offerings of community and school libraries, which open up additional layers of knowledge and nourish the spirit of inquiry. Access to a computer opens the door to further intellectual riches on the Internet. Admission to college brings with it the highest stage of access to the written word in the form of the university library, the resources of which are usually much more voluminous and varied than anything encountered previously. It also brings a much richer array of computer resources than those available in the home or high school.

In spite of the impressiveness of most campus libraries, however, many students remain unaware of the great diversity of materials and services they offer. Nor are they usually well grounded in navigating this complex array. Typical written assignments, such as term papers and book reviews, rarely require anything more than a few books from the library stacks. The procedure is simple and straightforward. Find some titles in the library catalog, jot down the call numbers, go to the shelves and collect them, and check them out. The selected volumes can be mined for information, including perhaps a few choice quotations. If additional material on a particular person or historical incident is needed, one of the large and authoritative encyclopedias in the library's reference room can be consulted. These days, students are also apt to resort to the Internet, perhaps even beginning their research there (some, alas, may end it there as well). Having filled up some note cards or notebooks during this process, the student uses them to write the paper. The library can then be ignored, except as a refuge of more or less quiet study, until the next such assignment.

The procedure just outlined may serve well enough for the requirements of some lower-division survey courses. Its shortcomings become painfully obvious, however, as soon as more advanced coursework is encountered. Therefore, a few of the notable deficiencies of this time-honored method of undergraduate research should be considered. First, it is probably directed at only one or two of several subject headings or keywords through which books on the topic might be located. Second, by being confined to the books the university library happens to possess, it ignores a vast and efficient interlibrary loan network that can obtain most published works on any topic within a couple of weeks. Third, it makes no attempt to access scholarly journals, with their wealth of information and new interpretations. It also ignores potentially valuable essays (or "chapters") on the topic that are not accessible by such a simple catalog search. Finally, it does not take into account the great variety of more specialized reference works that will prove helpful. These deficiencies can be corrected by learning about the resources offered by several vital library services often overlooked or underutilized by students: reference materials, periodicals, and the interlibrary loan system.

THE ONLINE LIBRARY CATALOG

Before examining these facilities, we should take a look back at a part of the library students already know (or think they know) how to use well: the Online Library Catalog. Often called OPAC (Online Public Access Catalog), this computerized system offers numerous benefits over the old card catalog. With only a few minutes required to learn the basics of the terminal, a complete search can be carried out from a single location. Moreover, terminals are increasingly found in convenient locations throughout the library and even on other parts of the campus. Most convenient of all, you can carry out an online catalog search from home on your computer. Furthermore, OPAC, in addition to listing the books and periodicals in your library, is the gateway to a large array of electronic resources.

Prior to embarking upon this electronic odyssey, it is important to know the object of the search. The selection and refinement of your topic is of course a critical matter. It may be assigned by your instructor, but usually the student is expected to develop his or her own topic, often within some defined parameters. Consultation with your instructor regarding the feasibility of your intended topic is always a good idea, but it should be realized that your topic will probably change during the course of your research. Usually this will be in the direction of limiting or pruning, since the original topic will many times be found to be overly broad. If, for example, your first idea was to write about nineteenth-century imperialism, you would have quickly discovered (or been told) that it was far too vast a subject. Seeking to limit it, you might have chosen British imperialism, German imperialism, or perhaps the "Scramble for Africa." These topics also proving unmanageable, you might have tried narrowing chronologically, geographically, or topically: e.g. "German involvement in east Africa, 1884–98" or "Cecil Rhodes and the expansion of the British Empire in south Africa, 1890–1902." However, delimiting your topic in this fashion requires that you already know something about imperialism or that you have started your research by reading some general work on the subject.

SUBJECT HEADINGS, KEYWORDS, AND TITLE WORDS

In the precomputer age, researchers were confined to looking for book titles through a card system in which items were arranged by Author, Title, and Subject. A researcher interested in a particular topic was heavily dependent upon the Subject Headings catalog, and substantial time was spent in determining what subject headings to use. Consulting the *Library of Congress Subject Headings*, a multivolume reference work, facilitated the process, but there was still considerable guesswork and frustration. While modern-day researchers should not expect instant results, the computer has made the location process much faster and easier. In OPAC the titles are arranged not only under the categories of Author, Title, and Subject, but also under Title Words (or Words in Title) and, frequently, by Keywords. In the latter two categories, you do not need to know the subject headings before you start searching. It is often advisable to use this method, as in many cases it will prove speedier, but before considering how to search by Title Words or Keywords, let us examine the more conventional approach using Author, Title, and Subject Headings.

You may start your research knowing that you want certain works that your instructor has mentioned or that you have seen referenced in your textbooks. The Author and the Title entries will provide the call numbers for these works, and the volumes can be garnered from the stacks, assuming of course that they are part of the library's holdings. Use of the Subject entries, however, requires more care and thought. Under which subject headings should you look? Several subject headings, perhaps as many as a dozen, will yield useful titles, but it is up to you to determine which one to look under. This is where it becomes important to spend some time analyzing your topic, thinking about the various subjects of which it forms a part. After all, very few of the books in your final bibliography will focus exactly on your topic.

Fortunately, the determination of subject headings is not a matter of guesswork. After spending a few minutes thinking about and jotting down some possible subject headings, you can always consult the above-mentioned *Library of Congress Subject Headings*. These reference volumes will allow you to discover what exact subject headings have been established in the classification system. With this information you can then go back to peruse the subject entries in the catalog and continue your search.

Now you will almost certainly be looking through a rather disparate range of subject headings. For example, if your topic is German imperialism in Africa, a couple of the useful subject headings turn out to be "Germany—Colonies—Africa" and "Germany—Colonies—History." As you begin to read some of the books on this topic, you might return to the subject catalog to search under the heading "Peters, Karl." This refers to the intrepid German explorer and empire-builder whose career bulks as large in the history of German East Africa as that of Cecil Rhodes does in the history of British South Africa. It is an example of how a number of topics turn out to have significant biographical components. Important information on your topic would thus be found in a biography of Peters. The reverse is also true. Having a biographical topic like Cecil Rhodes might seem to simplify the process: just copy down the entries under "Rhodes, Cecil" and you are through. But here, too, there will be a number of headings—important information about and interpretations of Rhodes are contained in studies of South Africa in the late nineteenth century, histories of Rhodesia, and accounts of the background of the Boer War.

At this point you may be wondering if all this means that you must somehow manage to determine all the subject headings for your topic in

order to compile a complete bibliography. The answer is no. Library cata-
loguers, in their infinite wisdom and mercy, have devised a useful system
of cross-referencing for the great majority of entries in OPAC. Let us say
that you had begun to research the history of women in the United States.
You would have learned from the *Library of Congress Subject Headings* that
one of the headings to use is "Women—United States—History." Enter-
ing this heading in the online catalog (you don't have to type the dashes,
just the words), you would find a number of potentially useful titles, including one that we encountered in Chapter One: June Sochen's *Herstory.*
When called up on the screen of a terminal at my university's library, the
bibliographic information for this book is as follows:

AUTHOR	Sochen, June, 1937–
TITLE	Herstory: a woman's view of American history/June Sochen.
PUBLISHER	New York : Alfred Pub. Co., [1974]
DESCRIPT	xiii, 448 p. : ill. ; 24 cm.
NOTES	Includes bibliographies and index.
SUBJECT	Women—United States—History.
	Minorities—United States.
	Women—United States—Social conditions.
	United States—Social conditions.
Books/4th floor	HQ1410 .S64 AVAILABLE
Books/4th floor	HQ1410 .S64 c. 2 AVAILABLE

In addition to the title, author, call number, date and place of publication, and the publisher, we are given other basic information: the book
has thirteen pages of front matter (note the Roman numeral xiii); 448
pages of text; and contains illustrations (note the "ill."); a bibliography,
and an index. We can also see that this particular library has two copies of
the book, neither of which is currently checked out. But it is the list of
subject headings under which this volume is indexed that is of special interest to us. (These are the four headings listed near the bottom of the
screen.) The first of them is the heading that was used to find this particular entry. The other three are headings under which Sochen's book can
also be located, along with other works likely to be of interest to you. Get
into the habit of jotting down the other subject headings (sometimes
there is only one) from each catalog entry you look up. Most online catalog systems make it extremely easy to check the listing under the other
subject headings. There will be a link on the screen labeled something like
"Show similar items" or "Show items with the same subject." When you

select this, you can then choose whichever of the other subject headings you wish, and quickly be shown a somewhat different range of titles (not only books, but other sources such as films, video tapes, CDs, etc.), some of which you may want to add to your bibliography.

Usually it is best to avoid starting with a Subject search altogether, and instead begin with a search by Title Words (sometimes called Words in Title, or Words) or by Keywords. The term Title Words is self-explanatory: a search by any word that appears in a book's title or subtitle. Keywords include words in subject headings as well as in titles. Let's say you are working on a paper on the employment of women in the United States during World War II, and that you know that there is a book with "Rosie the Riveter" in the title, or simply think it likely those words might be in the title of a book. By choosing the Title Words option, you could type "rosie" and "riveter" to call up the volume (there are actually several books with these words in the title). Here is the entry for one useful-sounding book, with call number and location information omitted:

AUTHOR	Honey, Maureen, 1945–
TITLE	Creating Rosie the Riveter: class, gender, and propaganda during World War II / Maureen Honey.
PUBLISHER	Amherst: University of Massachusetts Press, 1984.
DESCRIPT	x, 251 p. : ill. ; 24 cm.
NOTES	Includes index. Bibliography: p. [241]–248.
SUBJECT	Women—United States—History—20th century. Women in mass media—United States—History—20th century. Women—Employment—United States—History—20th century. World War, 1939–1945—Women—United States. Women—United States—Social conditions

Now you have five valuable subject headings under which to search, though the third and fourth seem to hold the most promise for a paper on this topic. You can now select the "Show similar items" from the menu, or, if the online catalog in your library doesn't have this feature, simply type in each of the subject headings you would like to use. The keywords function is an excellent means of jump-starting a search on any topic, and it is usually possible to guess what words are likely to appear in the title of a book on any given topic.

Another way to employ a Keyword or Title Word search to good effect is to think about possible titles of works with a somewhat wider scope than your topic. Very frequently, such works will have lengthy chapters, or perhaps entire sections, devoted to your topic. Thus, staying with the example of research for a paper on women during World War II, in addition to using words such as "Rosie the Riveter" that would lead you to titles more or less exactly on your subject, consider using words like "home front." Such a search will reveal a number of valuable works.[1]

Creating and Using a Research Bibliography

Another important habit to acquire early in the game is developing complete bibliography entries for all the titles that are obviously or even potentially of use to you in your research. You can either use 3 x 5 cards, or write the entries in a notebook and transfer them to your computer at the end of the day. Many OPAC systems give you the option of e-mailing the information on library materials to yourself, a process that facilitates making a bibliographic entry for each work on your computer. If you are searching from home via modem, or have a laptop computer with you at the library, you can enter the items directly into your computer, always making sure to save and back up your bibliography file frequently. There are also bibliographic software programs that make it easy to search out titles, download them to your computer, and format them in any of a number of ways that you specify. If you are using a card, write the author's or editor's name on the top line (last name first) with the title, publication data (place, publisher, date), and call number below. Thus the above entry, if written on a 3 x 5 card, would look like this:

> Honey, Maureen
> *Creating Rosie the Riveter: Class, Gender, and Propaganda during World War II.* Amherst: University of Massachusetts Press, 1984.
> H2 1420
> H66
> 1984

1 For example, Allan Winkler, *Home Front U.S.A.: America during World War II*, 2nd ed. (Wheeling, Ill.: Harlan Davidson, 2001).

When you enter titles into a computer, hit the Return key only when you are moving on to the next book, article, or essay. That way, you can use the sort or alphabetizing function of your word-processing application, which will instantly arrange your entries alphabetically by authors' last names. Thus the above entry should be entered into a computer as follows:

Honey, Maureen. *Creating Rosie the Riveter: Class, Gender, and Propaganda during World War II.* Amherst: University of Massachusetts Press, 1984.

Note that on the handwritten card the title of the book is underlined, which is the convention for showing items that will be italicized in print. When you enter the same information in the computer, there is no point in underlining—just use the italicizing function that every word-processing application contains. Also, in making computer entries, use the paragraph formatting function of your word processor for indenting the second and subsequent lines rather than the Tab key. Using tabs will produce problems if you later change font size or margins, or if you make any changes in wording. As you build up your bibliography file, keep it alphabetized so that you can tell at a glance if you already have an entry on a particular book. Even if you are working directly from an alphabetized computer bibliographic file, you should always have a hard copy of it on hand. You will probably also find it useful to make brief notations on your bibliography cards or computer hard copy, on such matters as the particular library in which you found the book and whether you have already read or at least looked at it; brief annotations on its contents will also prove helpful.

Once your project is launched, always have your card file (or the hard copy of your computerized bibliography file) with you when you enter the library, or when you go online for further research. As you access the stacks using the catalog, new titles will loom into view frequently. One of the ways this happens may already be familiar to you—it is called "shelf browsing." This entails simply looking at the volumes adjacent to those books you have gone to the stacks to fetch; some of your target book's neighbors are almost certain to prove valuable. Many online systems have a menu option that lets you "shelf browse" electronically. Another important method of adding titles to your bibliography is mining the bibliographies of the books you already have found. As soon as you get your hands on a new volume, examine its bibliography for other sources you do not know about yet. One of the advantages of this method is that it will let you identify wanted titles that your library does not have in its holdings, many of which can then be obtained through interlibrary loan or by going to another library.

Published Bibliographies

Another very effective means of finding useful titles is to consult published bibliographies available in book, article, or essay form. Sometimes good bibliographies on your topic are available on the Internet. It may indeed be advisable to begin your search in this fashion. I have deferred discussing this resource until now because I think it essential to start with some knowledge of the organization of the library catalog. Also, consulting a published bibliography on your topic at the outset might tend to short circuit your search and thus interfere with learning some basic research procedures. Bear in mind, too, that even if you find a comprehensive published bibliography exactly on your topic, it is not going to include any titles published after it went to press, which is often a year or more prior to its publication date. Thus, even with a recently published bibliography in hand, you must still search elsewhere in order to find the most recent books, articles, and essays on your topic. And don't assume that a bibliography you find online contains the latest materials; quite apart from questions of quality (a particular concern with Internet resources), it may have been a considerable time since that web site was created or updated.

In addition to those scholars who write histories or edit primary source materials, others provide a most valuable service by collecting and publishing bibliographies on various subjects. These are intended as guides to researchers and provide a list of books and articles on a given subject, with entries often arranged under subtopics and sometimes annotated. (Annotations are the editor's comments and indicate something about the scope and usefulness of each entry.) When these research guides are written as essays rather than simply lists of titles, they are called bibliographic essays.

Bibliographies can be located in a number of ways. The subject index of the catalog is one such method. When you have discovered an appropriate heading for your topic, look at the headings immediately following it to see if there is one with the word "Bibliography" added. It will be recalled that for research on the history of American women, one of the key headings is "Women—United States—History." Immediately following is the subject heading "Women—United States—History—Bibliography." Here will be found the titles of a number of valuable bibliographies on this topic or some portion of it. An example is Jill K. Conway, *The Female Experience in Eighteenth- and Nineteenth-Century America: A Guide to the History of American Women* (New York: Garland Pub., 1982). Conway's bibliography lists the titles of thousands of books, articles, and collections of primary sources on various facets of the history of American women. Remember, however, that a great deal has been published on this topic since Conway's bibliography, so you still need to undertake a full search using the methods described in this chapter. It is a good idea whenever looking up something in the subject headings in OPAC to see if there is also a bibliography heading for your topic. The same holds true for finding primary sources. If there are published sources for your topic in the library there will be a heading in the subject index with the word "Sources" added. Look, for example, under the heading "Women—United States—History—Sources."

In the reference room of your library are other ways to access bibliographies. There are even several good "bibliographies of bibliographies," which list bibliographies in all fields. A valuable one for historical researchers is Robert Balay, ed., *Guide to Reference Books*, 11th ed. (Chicago: American Library Association, 1996), a work that is regularly revised and updated. By looking up the entries under history and the appropriate subheading, you will find references to bibliographic works on your topic, or on the field of history of which your topic is a part. One particularly valuable bibliographic reference tool for historical researchers in all fields is Mary Beth Norton, ed., *The American Historical Association Guide to Historical Literature* (New York: Oxford University Press, 1995).

A good method of finding relevant titles your library may not have is to consult the subject index of *Books in Print*, a multivolume reference work that is frequently updated and is also available online. Whether using the electronic or printed form it is always a good idea to check every few weeks to see if any new items have been added under your subject's heading. The practice of examining the latest printed supplements or the computerized databases to check for additions to the body of scholarship on your topic applies as well to the other indexes and abstracts, which we will now consider—those that provide access to articles and book reviews in scholarly journals as well as essays in books.

PRINTED AND ELECTRONIC INDEXES AND ABSTRACTS

In the last chapter we saw the importance of scholarly journals in the process of historical revisionism. Scholarly articles are not mere adjuncts to books; they are efficient vehicles for presenting various kinds of special studies as well as the initial form in which historians often challenge existing interpretations. It is therefore vitally important to find and read the relevant periodical literature. There are a number of indexing and abstracting resources available online for this purpose; some will also lead you to additional book titles as well as to book reviews. Most of them are published quarterly and bound into volumes at the end of each year along with a comprehensive index of the year's issues. Some publications provide five- or ten-year indexes to facilitate research. Whether using the online database or the published index, when you first consult each of these reference works, spend a few minutes acquainting yourself with their internal organization and determine which subject headings are used for your topic. If you are using an online database, check to see how far back in time (by publication dates of your sources) it goes; it may index only materials published in the last ten years or so. If this is the case, you will have to used the published form of the index if you need to locate materials older than that. When using the published index, start with the most recent date and work your way backward in time.

How far back in time you go depends upon your topic, the kind of paper you are preparing to write, and the guidelines set by your instructor. Keep in mind that, unlike the situation in the sciences, engineering, or medicine, the older literature in the field of history does not necessarily become "obsolete." Furthermore, when preparing a historiographic essay, which is, after all, a history of the history-writing on your topic, you will necessarily need to have older titles as well as the more recent ones. The indexes, abstracts, and other finding aids discussed in the following pages are also, for convenience, listed in Appendices A and B. These can function as handy checklists when you are carrying out your research on a particular topic.

Many students will already be somewhat familiar with the *Readers' Guide to Periodical Literature*. This widely used published and online reference work is a good index to popular publications, but a glance at the list of magazines at the front of any volume of the *Readers' Guide* (or the list that you can access online) reveals very few scholarly journals. Accessing articles on your topics that appear in the vast majority of the historical journals requires the use of indexes that are more specialized and scholarly. A good starting point is the *Humanities Index* (called *Humanities Full Text* in its online form), which indexes most of the major English-language historical journals. This is one of many indexes published by the W. W. Wilson Co., and, depending upon the electronic set-up in your library, it may be available (back to a certain point in time) as part of the

WilsonWeb database. Be sure to prepare a card or computer entry for each article you find, including all the essential bibliographic information: author, title, name of journal, volume, date, and page numbers. If for example, you were writing a paper on King Louis XIV of France, you would find a reference to an article in Volume 18 of *French Historical Studies*. A card on this item would read as follows:

> Smith, Jay M.
> "'Our Sovereign's Gaze': Kings, Nobles, and State Formation in Seventeenth-Century France." *French Historical Studies* 18 (Fall 1993): 396–415.

The example above is of a handwritten card. The volume number of *French Historical Studies* in which this article appears is 18; the inclusive page numbers of the article are 396 to 415. Note that abbreviations like "vol." (for Volume) or "pp." (for pages) are no longer used. This entry in your computer, in the same format as the final printed bibliography at the end of your completed paper, and substituting italicizing for underlining, would look like this:

Smith, Jay M. "'Our Sovereign's Gaze': Kings, Nobles, and State Formation in Seventeenth-Century France." *French Historical Studies* 18 (Fall 1993): 396–415.

There are a number of more specialized indexes to periodical literature that, depending on your topic, may be of interest to you. For any topic in British or European history, the *British Humanities Index* is apt to prove useful. The *Hispanic American Periodicals Index* is invaluable for any facet of Latin American history or the history of Hispanics in the United States. Those researching any aspect of the history of law will want to consult the *Index to Legal Periodicals*. The law journals indexed in the latter are, for the most part, not found in the other indexes. (Some of the articles in law journals are of a historical character and are important vehicles for launching revisionist interpretations.) Other indexes that may prove valuable to historical researchers are the *Biography Index*, the *Art Index*, the *Music Index*, and *Index Medicus*.

The various indexes we have discussed are vital and indispensable, but most of them do not provide anything beyond titles, authors, and bibliographic citations. From this basic information you must try to determine whether a particular article is necessary for your research. If the journal in which the article appears is part of your library's holdings, this may pose no particular problem. But what if it is not, and you want to know whether it is worth getting a copy of the article through interlibrary loan? Some online databases and published indexes provide details about the content of the articles; these are referred to as abstracts. The organization of the material is very similar to indexes which give only the bibliographic particulars, but more information is provided—after each entry there is a description of the scope and contents of the article. This does not mean, however, that you can ignore the more bare-bones indexes and go straight to the ones that offer abstracts. A quite different range of scholarly journals is covered by the abstracts, and the most widely available set of abstracts for European and world history covers only from the Renaissance to the present. Even for modern history you would miss some important articles, since some of the journals covered in the more restrictive indexes are not covered by those that provide abstracts. These are simply some of the quirks in the organization of the materials for historical research.

The two most important abstracts for our purposes are *Historical Abstracts* and *America: History and Life*.[2] The first is for world history and European history from the Renaissance to the present, while the latter is concerned with American history. Like other indexes, these abstracts are available in both printed and electronic form. If your library has them in the latter form, remember to check to see how far back it goes. The structure and arrangement of the printed abstracts are somewhat different from the other indexes, so spend a little time orienting yourself before commencing your search. It will be noticed that each of them is organized into several parts, including article abstracts and citations, an index to book reviews, a bibliography of books, articles, and dissertations, and an annual index. In the electronic form, the categories are combined in the index, and you can limit your search by document type (book, article, etc.), by time period, and other categories. When you call up a screen, it will indicate whether the item is a book, article, dissertation, or book review. The subject headings will be different from those encountered so far, because now you are dealing with exclusively historical materials. Thus, for example, you will find no heading with "History" appended to

---

2 *Dissertation Abstracts International* is also very useful, but since it is cross-indexed in both *Historical Abstracts* and *America: History and Life*, it is not necessary to search through it directly. If you come across an entry in either *Historical Abstracts* or *America: History and Life* with the code DAI affixed, copy down the volume and abstract number, then look it up in *Dissertation Abstracts International*. Many dissertations can be ordered on interlibrary loan.

it. Nor will "United States" be added to subject headings in *America: History and Life.*

Also notice how very different are the journals listed in the abstracts from those covered by the indexes; it is a much longer list and includes many journals of local history. In *America: History and Life*, for example, you will note a very large number of publications concerned with state and local history, like the *Utah Historical Quarterly*, the *Pennsylvania Magazine of Biography and History*, the *Southern California Quarterly*, and *Chicago History*. You might think that these journals would be of little use to you unless your topic happened to be concerned with the state or city in question. But remember, from our discussion of secondary works in the last chapter, that important revisionist scholarship often appears in the form of local studies. Thus if you were writing about the Freedmen's Bureau, that subject heading in *America: History and Life* would lead you to the title and abstract of an article by James Stealey in the journal *West Virginia History* with the title of "The Freedmen's Bureau in West Virginia." The bibliographic information and the accompanying abstract are displayed in the following fashion:

17 A: 1135. Stealey, James Edmund III. THE FREEDMEN'S BUREAU IN WEST VIRGINIA. *West Virginia History* 1978 39(2–3): 99–142. During 1865–68 the Freedmen's Bureau was active in Berkeley and Jefferson counties, West Virginia, where freedmen were a fifth of the population. The young army officers in charge were zealous for the blacks' welfare but did not have much success in protecting their legal rights. The establishment of schools met a mixed white reception, especially where the black attendance was large; the Bureau's most significant effort was in the founding of Storer College, a Negro normal school. Based on Freedmen's Bureau records and other primary and secondary sources; 216 notes. J. H. Broussard.

The information provided here will help you decide whether to add this title to your bibliography. If your paper were on the educational activities of the Freedmen's Bureau, you certainly would want it. Note also that this is quite a lengthy article based on research in the primary sources and has a large number of footnotes or endnotes. J. H. Broussard wrote the abstract. If you decide to use it, fill out a bibliography entry and submit an interlibrary loan request (unless, of course, your library has *West Virginia History* in its holdings). Note that the format of the abstract is a little different from the one you should use for making a bibliography card or computer entry. In your records the above item should be rendered as:

Stealey, James Edmund III. "The Freedmen's Bureau in West Virginia."
   West Virginia History 39 (1978): 99–142.

Article titles go in quotation marks, not caps, while the name of a journal
(*West Virginia History*) is italicized (underlined on a handwritten bibliog-
raphy card). The volume number is 39, the page numbers are 99 to 142.
The issue number (2–3 in this example) is unnecessary.

Finding Scholarly Essays

The procedures just described should guide you efficiently to the articles
in scholarly journals. But how does one find the scholarly essays (or chapters) that appear in books with titles that give little or no clue to the specialized nature of the essays they contain? This is the problem of the "hidden literature" referred to in Chapter Two. The answer is to consult that
highly useful reference source, the *Essay and General Literature Index*. Organized like the other indexes, and available both online and in print, it
provides access to the titles of essays that appear in books. For example, if
your topic were the economic aspect of decolonization in Africa, you
would find under the subject heading "Africa" in the *Essay and General
Literature Index* a reference to an essay by Jean Suret-Canale titled "From
Colonization to Independence in French Tropical Africa: The Economic
Background," in a book with the title of *The Transfer of Power in Africa*.
Deciding that this definitely would be useful, you proceed to fill out a
bibliography card, or an entry in your computerized bibliography, as follows before proceeding to look up the book in the library catalog under
the title or the name of one of the editors:

> Suret-Canale, Jean
> "From Colonization to Independence in French Tropical
> Africa: The Economic Background." In *The Transfer of Power
> in Africa: Decolonization, 1940–1960*, 445–81. Edited by
> Prosser Gifford and William Roger Louis. New Haven: Yale
> University Press, 1982.

This same item in your computerized bibliography is:

Suret-Canale, Jean. "From Colonization to Independence in French
   Tropical Africa: The Economic Background." In *The Transfer of
   Power in Africa: Decolonization, 1940–1960*, 445–81. Edited by

Prosser Gifford and William Roger Louis. New Haven: Yale University Press, 1982.

If you need to order this item on interlibrary loan, be sure you request it by the title of the book, not of the essay, and that you list Prosser Gifford and William Roger Louis as the authors, though they are in fact the editors of the volume.

OTHER IMPORTANT DATABASES

In addition to the databases and published indexes described above, there are others that make available a huge array of titles of books, articles, essays, and conference papers, as well as newspaper articles and a variety of reference materials. One of the most valuable of them is *WorldCat*—the combined catalogued holdings of thousands of libraries, searchable by keywords as well as subject headings, author, and title. This is an excellent means of finding books on your topic that your own university library does not have. In many cases, you can submit your request electronically from the same screen on which you found the book, by using the "Order" command. This sends a request to the interlibrary loan office in your library, which in turn orders the book for you. It is not necessary, by the way, for you to note where the needed volume is located, only that it exists. The staff in your interlibrary loan office (or document delivery, or whatever it is called on your campus) will order it, usually electronically, from the location from which delivery is apt to be the speediest. Because there is always some delay involved in procuring items through interlibrary loan, it is vitally important to get an early start on your bibliographic search.

One caveat about *WorldCat* is that it is so enormous that, just using a basic keyword search, you are very likely to encounter thousands of titles of all kinds of materials—clearly an unmanageable situation. The way to avoid this is to select the option for Advanced Search or Expert Search. This allows you to limit your search according to such criteria as language, document type, year of publication, and so on. Another caveat is that not all of the books you find on *WorldCat* can be obtained through interlibrary loan. Some are in restricted circulation at the libraries that hold them.[3]

3 Many universities belong to a regional consortium of libraries, such as the Link Plus system in California, with mutual borrowing privileges and a streamlined interlibrary loan system. This is frequently the most convenient and efficient way of obtaining books not in your library's holdings.

Another database especially useful for historical researchers is *ArticleFirst*. As with *WorldCat*, using the Advanced Search or Expert Search is a good idea. Also like *WorldCat*, the item (in this case an article or book review) can be requested electronically on interlibrary loan by using the "Order" command at the bottom of the screen. Before submitting a request, however, double check to make sure your library does not have the item. In the case of an article or book review, this means checking to see if your library has not only the journal but the specific volume number of the journal in which the needed item appears—many libraries have only certain volumes of any given periodical. There is a very handy "Lib" command at the bottom of the screen in *ArticleFirst* and *WorldCat*. This will display the libraries that have the item—or rather, it will display an alphabetical listing of code letters for the libraries that have the item. Find out the code for your library—if it does not appear on the screen, just submit an interlibrary loan request.

A few other good databases for historical researchers should be noted. One is *OmniFile Full Text Mega*, which, like *Humanities Full Text* and the *Essay and General Literature* Index (both referred to above), are part of the WilsonWeb cluster of databases. The names of some of these databases may give the impression that the articles you find in them will be full text, rather than just bibliographic citations. This is true of some of the articles you will find by this means, but for the most part you will be given simply the bibliographic citation. With the passage of time, more and more materials will be available in full text form, but for the foreseeable future, you will have to acquire most articles by the more traditional means already discussed. Two more valuable databases are *Academic Search Elite* and *World History Full Text*, both part of the EBSCO cluster of databases. As with all databases, the interface will vary from library to library. In some cases, they will be listed directly in alphabetical fashion, while in others you will have to click on WilsonWeb, or whatever cluster in which the database you need is included.

Historical Research on the Internet

The Internet has undergone extraordinary expansion in the last few years, and many web sites are quite valuable to historical researchers. They offer an array of primary and secondary sources, along with archives of historic maps, photographs, and other images. A web address is known as an URL (Universal Resource Locator). Most begin with "http," which stands for hypertext transfer protocol. This is the system that makes possible the linkages from one web page to others. Highlighted or underlined items can be opened by pointing with the mouse and clicking on the item. When you find a particular site useful, you will no doubt want to return to it, so remember to bookmark it. Having established a bookmark for this site, you can access it again quickly through the pull-down menu on your browser.

Since many web sites are ephemeral, while others frequently change their URLs, it would be pointless to list specific sites here.[4] The important thing is to be effective in searching for web sites on your topic. There are a number of good search engines available, such as Google and Yahoo, which will lead you to useful material. The problem is assessing the importance of the many hits, perhaps hundreds, that might be returned by a typical search. The Internet is a vast, uncoordinated arena where the good sites are generally outnumbered by those that are worthless, occasionally vicious, or just focused on selling something, though the major search engines are considerably improved. A few years ago an Internet search for "Hitler" would have turned up a few really valuable hits buried among a host of sites organized by neo-Nazi cultists, sellers of Third Reich memorabilia, and Holocaust deniers. The junk sites are still out there, but, on the whole, the search engines do a much better job of listing the valuable sites near the top of their lists. Still, Internet research requires that you choose your search terms with some care. You may need to try a number of alternatives before hitting on the right ones. When confronted with a large number of hits after even a careful search, try to make what critical assessments you can from the description of each site on the list. One good way to minimize the problem is to use a search engine that is focused on sites of educational value. Check to see if your library has *NetFirst* among its databases. A *NetFirst* search is certain to return mostly useful hits.

There is certainly a rapidly expanding array of riches available to historical researchers on the Internet. In spite of this abundance, the number of these online sources is still dwarfed by the huge number of sources available in print, and this is likely to remain true for a long time. Think of the history sites on the Internet as a valuable adjunct to printed sources and other media, not a substitute for them.

4 One helpful published guide is Dennis A. Trinkle and Scott A. Merriman, eds., *The History Highway 2000: A Guide to Internet Resources,* 2nd ed. (Armonk, NY: M.E. Sharpe, 2000).

FINDING USEFUL REFERENCE MATERIALS

During the researching and writing of any paper, it is necessary to look up certain key facts or dates and acquire additional background information about a particular event or person. Reference materials, including encyclopedias, dictionaries, atlases, chronologies, and the like are indispensable. Some of these items, especially the more general encyclopedias, are readily available online.[5] For the most part, however, the more specialized reference materials you will require in your work are in printed form. Many of them will be available in the reference room of your library; others are shelved in the regular stacks. There are also some good published guides to reference material.[6]

At an early stage of your research, you should reconnoiter the reference room, since there are important variations from library to library. In some, for example, all the atlases will be found together, regardless of the part of the world or time period they cover. Maybe all the biographical materials will be grouped together without regard to geographic region or historical era. Many libraries will aggregate their reference materials on much the same system as the books in the stacks; knowing the call number range of most of the books in your bibliography, you can shelf browse the same section in the reference room. Once you understand the layout, you will quickly discover a number of important and often fascinating reference tools. As you do, be sure to jot down the title and call number of each (or its location in the reference room) on a card. And don't hesitate to ask a reference librarian for help—both in finding relevant reference works and in using them.

Reference works can of course be located through the keyword or subject headings of the library catalog. But shelf browsing is apt to be particularly effective, especially if the materials in the reference room have the same call number ranges as the books in the stacks on the same topics. If, for example, your topic is some aspect of the Spanish Civil War, you will notice that many of the call numbers of the books you have found start with DP (assuming that your library uses the Library of Congress classification system). DP is the classification for Spanish history. If you go to the DPs in the reference room, you will possibly discover a highly

5 An excellent gateway to a large range of such materials is at www.refdesk.com.
6 See, for example, *Reference Sources in History: An Introductory Guide,* ed. Ronald H. Fritze, Brian E. Cutts, and Louis A. Vyhnanek (Santa Barbara: ABC-CLIO, 1990).

useful *Historical Dictionary of the Spanish Civil War, 1936–1939.*[7] This volume provides a wealth of information on the major and minor figures of that conflict, plus descriptions of major parties, campaigns, and battles. There is a similar reference work on the Vietnam War, with entries for all the battles, campaigns, and major persons involved, plus a detailed chronology of events.[8] Those working in ancient history will find the nearly 1,200 pages of entries in *The New Century Classical Handbook* invaluable.[9] The reference room holds a great diversity of materials of interest to historians, such as biographical dictionaries of every conceivable kind, encyclopedias (both general and specialized), atlases, almanacs, and official guides to various countries. Indexes to book reviews, such as the *Book Review Index* and the *Index to Book Reviews in Historical Periodicals,* are also likely to prove serviceable. The best way to find out what is available in your library's reference room is to take some time to go on an exploratory journey around it.

The reference materials cited above are only a tiny sample of the riches that lie waiting in the reference room and elsewhere. Whatever kind of paper you are writing and whatever its topic, there are bound to be reference materials of vital importance to you. Used intelligently in harness with your primary and secondary sources, they will both deepen your understanding and lighten your labors. Keep the holdings of the reference room in mind as we move through the next two chapters, on writing a historiographic essay and writing a research paper.

7 Edited by James W. Cortada (London: Greenwood Press, 1982). This is an example of a "split footnote," one in which part of the information regarding a publication—in this case the title— is given in the text, with the rest of the data in the footnote.
8 *The Vietnam War: An Almanac,* edited by John S. Bowman, with an introduction by Fox Butterfield (New York: World Almanac Publications, 1985).
9 Edited by Catherine B. Avery (New York: Appleton-Century-Croft, 1962).

CHAPTER FOUR

Exploring Changing Interpretations: The Historiographic Essay

In this chapter we will explore more fully the nature of the revisionist process by considering the writing of a historiographic essay. In Chapter One we examined a few of the major currents of historiography in the broadest sense of the word—that is, the history of history writing. Our concern now will be with historiography in its narrower meaning—the variety of approaches, methods, and interpretations employed by historians on a particular topic. The historiographic essay is an important literary form in its own right, providing the reader with a sense of how the topic he or she is interested in has already been approached by previous scholars. An awareness of the historiography on your topic is an essential prerequisite to undertaking research and writing using primary sources. Knowing the kinds of approaches and interpretations already employed by others, as well as the still unanswered questions on your topic, can help direct your inquiry along original lines. The writing of a historiographic essay is also an excellent learning exercise, since in order to write one, it is necessary to become immersed in the intellectual processes of historians as they modify and revise our view of the past.

Selecting and Refining a Topic

Selecting and refining a topic is vitally important. Many students are inclined to choose a particularly vivid historical incident like the Japanese attack on Pearl Harbor or the assassination of Abraham Lincoln in the belief that it will prove both interesting and manageable. In this they are not deceived. The intrinsic human drama of such events, as well as their being limited to short and specific spans of time, makes them attractive research topics to the busy undergraduate. This is no doubt a major reason why a topic in military history is often a first choice. Another is that in many cases the survey courses students have encountered emphasize military conflicts and the more dramatic political events. Indeed, many of these are quite suitable subjects for a historiographic essay, since they have been approached and interpreted by historians in a variety of ways. But before seizing too readily on one of the more "famous" topics, it is worth your while to ponder the many alternatives open to you.

For example, there is a great abundance of fascinating subjects in social history, each with a rich and varied historiography. Numerous books, articles, and essays have been written on aspects of the history of education, sexuality, trade unions, sports, religion, immigration, popular entertainment, and crime. The history of science, technology, or industry can also provide viable and interesting topics. You may feel a bit uncomfortable selecting a less familiar topic, but doing so will offer you greater opportunities for expanding your intellectual horizons. Even if you choose a biographical topic, it need not concern a well-known political or military figure. Many thousands of fascinating people in all fields of endeavor throughout history have been the subject of significant scholarly attention.

The initial selection of a topic usually needs to be followed by a process of refining. Frequently the subject as it is first conceptualized turns out to be too broad; occasionally it is too narrow. You would soon discover, for example, that a topic like "Renaissance Humanism" is extraordinarily vast and complex. It has such an extensive literature that you could not hope to find, read, and analyze more than a tiny fraction of it within the time constraints of your course and the space limitations of your paper. Even a reduction in the scope of the topic to "Renaissance Humanism in Florence" would still be too broad, though such a geographic narrowing of the subject is moving you toward something manageable. In addition to this geographic focus, you could also limit the scope of your paper topically, chronologically, or biographically. A combination of these methods of narrowing is exemplified in a research paper title like "The Medici and Civic Humanism in Fifteenth-Century Florence." Even this topic may require additional refinement, but clearly it is much more viable than the first choice, or even the second. The precise scope of your paper probably will not be defined until you have gained a clearer notion of the dimensions of the topic's historiography.

RESEARCH FOR A HISTORIOGRAPHIC ESSAY: A CASE STUDY

The finding of historical sources was described in general terms in the last chapter; now we will examine the process as it applies to a specific topic. The example we will consider is an essay of about 4,500 words written by Patricia J. Autran, a student in my History Methods class.[1] The assignment was to write a historiographic essay of approximately twenty pages based on fifteen to twenty secondary sources. Her paper is titled "The Lewis and Clark Expedition: Changing Interpretations." This essay serves well as an example, since it cuts across a number of important topics in American history—exploration, westward expansion, scientific inquiry, encounters with indigenous peoples, the role of women, and attitudes towards the natural environment, to name a few. It also obviously has important biographical dimensions, including not only Meriwether Lewis and William Clark, but such figures as Thomas Jefferson, who envisaged and launched the enterprise, and Sacagawea, the Native American woman who helped guide it.

In searching for books on this topic, the initial step is the logical one of doing a library catalog search using the keywords "lewis and clark." Depending upon the extent of your library's holdings, this step alone should take you to dozens, perhaps even hundreds of titles. Having hit such a large number of titles can produce a sinking feeling. How can you be expected to winnow this down to a manageable number of titles, especially considering that these are just the books? You still have to search for articles and essays. Be of good cheer—the challenge is not as formidable as it appears. The key is to keep your reserach focused and systematic. The first thing to do is to keep in mind that you are looking for secondary works. Scrolling through the list of sources quickly shows that many of the titles are various editions of the journals of Lewis and Clark. They are primary sources—essential reading if you are undertaking a paper about the expedition itself, but remember: you are writing about the historians and the different ways they have approached and interpreted the topic. Therefore you should consider only the secondary sources on the list. You can further exclude anything that is described on the catalog entry as "Juvenile Literature." The list is already considerably shorter, and not much time has been expended. What next?

Since the assignment is a historiographic essay, and therefore you want to explore as many different kinds of interpretations as possible, let that concern guide your further winnowing of sources. Titles and sub-

1 I wish to express my gratitude to Ms. Autran for permission to reproduce her paper.

titles of books will usually give you a good idea of their scope and approach. Try to select works with as many approaches to the topic as possible. From the titles, it will be evident that some works are general in character, others have a biographical focus, while others deal with topics like the scientific observations of the expedition, relations with Native Americans, and so on. This provides a basis for further selection, but at this point you need to go to the library stacks to have a look at the volumes you have identified for possible inclusion in your bibliography. Examining the books for apparent depth, scholarly rigor, and interpretive interest may take some time, and involves looking at such matters as bibliographies, footnotes, and possibly even the author's academic credentials. This may not help you much in deciding between one scholarly book and another when drastic pruning is called for, but at least it should be possible to exclude works that are clearly superficial and unscholarly.

At this point you would be well advised to look at some impressive recent scholarly book on the subject to see which secondary sources that author considers important. Perhaps in perusing the list of authors in your catalog search, you recognized the name Stephen E. Ambrose, one of America's leading historians. Among his many books is *Undaunted Courage: Meriwether Lewis, Thomas Jefferson, and the Opening of the American West* (1996). Even if you had not heard of him, a perusal of his volume in the stacks would make his book's value evident. Examining the titles in the bibliography of his book, and perhaps also looking to see which sources he frequently cites in his endnotes, will assist you in further refining your selection of titles for your bibliography. (In addition to this, you should also check out the Ambrose volume and begin reading it, because you need to acquire more factual knowledge of the topic in order to complete your search for titles). One very likely result of perusing Ambrose's bibliography is that it will bring to your attention important sources that your library does not have in its holdings. These can be ordered through interlibrary loan. You also should search any database of libraries affiliated with your own to find titles that your library does not possess. *WorldCat* (described in the previous chapter) might also be helpful, though it is such a massive database that a simple search under "lewis and clark" is likely to produce thousands of hits. On the other hand, a "sacagawea" search in *WorldCat* is sure to produce a more manageable list of titles. When using *WorldCat*, always remember to use the search-reducing features described in the previous chapter.

In the search for scholarly articles on this topic, the online database (or the bound volume index) *America: History and Life* will prove especially valuable. *The Humanities Index* (either online as part of the Wilson-Web or in bound-volume format) and the *ArticleFirst* database should also yield some good titles. Depending on the array of databases available in your library, other indexes and abstracts may also prove useful. This includes some full-text databases such as *J-Stor*. By giving you immediate access to the complete article online, full-text databases will save time, especially if the article is in a journal that your library does not have in its holdings. Fortunately, even when a full-text version of the article is not available to you online and your library does not have the journal in question, the interlibrary loan department can usually obtain a copy of the article for you in relatively short time. In addition to journal articles, don't forget the "hidden literature" (essays or chapters on the topic that are parts of books rather than journals). The *Essay and General Literature Index* (online or bound volume) is essential for this purpose. The footnotes and endnotes of the articles and essays you locate should also be examined for possible further additions to your bibliography.

Once you have reduced your sources to a manageable number (in this case, the guidelines called for a maximum of twenty titles), you are ready to read and take notes. Your reading must necessarily be approached somewhat differently than for an ordinary term paper, where you are reading to extract information about the topic itself. Remember, your focus should be on what the historians are doing. In order to extract this kind of information, it is necessary to read the sources with the purpose of the essay in mind: to inform the reader of some of the major writings on the topic, how these works differ from one another, and how the historiography evolves over time. Titles, as we have seen, usually give us some idea of the author's plan. Taking a look at tables of contents, prefaces, introductions, and conclusions is another way to get a quick fix on an author's orientation. If you do this before actually reading the work (and it is not always necessary to read every work in its entirety), you will be much better able to look for and find especially significant passages that reveal the author's approach or methodology. As you do so, take notes on 5 x 8 or 4 x 6 inch notecards, including precise page references to passages you may wish to cite or quote. The same care must be given to taking full and precise notecards of your reading as that given to your bibliography card file. It is also possible to take notes on your computer, but, if so, you must devise a good method of grouping those entries that relate to the same topic. There are software products on the market that facilitate this. One clear advantage of computerized notes is that when you are writing the paper, it is easy, if you have taken good notes, to copy and paste for quotations. You may, however, find that filling out cards by hand turns out to be simpler. While the computer makes both bibliographic searching and writing vastly more efficient than the old methods, its advantage when it comes to notetaking is by no means so clear cut.

WRITING THE HISTORIOGRAPHIC ESSAY

Now we can turn to the writing of a historiographic essay on this subject. It is crucial to remember that this paper will not be a history of the Lewis and Clark Expedition, but rather an account of how historians have written about the topic. Of course, a number of facts concerning Lewis and Clark will be introduced into the essay, but they are used to illustrate the approaches and findings of the various authors. When writing a historiographic essay, a good method to use is to think of yourself as preparing a guide to the historiography for a fellow student who knows a little about the period but has a very limited knowledge of the topic. The introduction to the paper can therefore provide some facts about the Lewis and Clark Expedition in order to remind or inform the reader of some basic features of the topic. Consider how the opening paragraphs in Patricia Autran's historiographic essay establish this foundation and conclude with a "bridge" to the discussion of the historians who have written about Lewis and Clark, which forms the body of the paper. Note that quotations from the secondary sources being discussed are either set off by quotation marks, or, for longer passages, given in block quotation form without quotation marks. Some quotations of less than a sentence are grafted onto the author's sentence, making a "run-in" quotation. These types of quotations, along with other aspects of the essay, are pointed out in the marginal comments. (For more on quotations, see the section on quoting in the next chapter). Further observations on how this essay is constructed follow the essay, and are also to be found in the marginal comments. Endnote references can be found immediately following the text of the essay.

******

"*Ocian*[1] in View! O! the joy."[2] These words were written on November 6, 1805 by the jubilant William Clark upon reaching the goal of one of the most dramatic undertakings in American history. Long before the acquisition of the Louisiana Territory in 1803, President Thomas Jefferson had begun planning for the exploration of this enormous area that no American citizen had ever traversed. Jefferson, who had long been fascinated by the unknown territory, hoped that the exploration would lead to a discovery of a river route capable of carrying trading goods from the Mississippi River to the Pacific Ocean. The Louisiana Purchase facilitated the enterprise and gave the President a sense of urgency to begin the exploration as soon as possible. Captains Meriwether Lewis and William Clark[3] led the Corps of Discovery on an exciting and hazardous journey that began in May 1804 and lasted twenty-eight months, ending with their return to St. Louis in September 1806.

Intro-duction providing basic facts about the Lewis and Clark expedition

In addition to discovering a water route from the Mississippi to the Pacific, the expedition had several other important purposes. Lewis and Clark were to make a complete scientific survey of the regions along the route of the Missouri River, across the Rocky Mountains, down the Columbia River, and finally to the Pacific Ocean. They were to determine the longitude and latitude of the area, analyze and describe plant and animal life, and report on the culture of the native peoples that they encountered. Most importantly, they were asked to evaluate the possibilities of trade and agriculture in that region.

During the journey, Lewis and Clark produced eight detailed volumes, ranging from maps, climate, geography, and ethnic observations to the descriptions of new species of plants and animals. Their journals also included a dramatic day by day story of the adventures and hardships experienced by the group. The information contained in the volumes would be studied and analyzed for the next two centuries. Historians produced many books, articles and essays using the material from the volumes. Over time, each writer has interpreted and approached the history of the Lewis and Clark Expedition in a different manner and each has attempted to meet a particular historiographical goal.

Trans-ition to discussion of histor-iography of the topic

Although the writing of the expedition's history began soon after the volumes were released, this essay will focus on those works produced during the last half century or so. Most of the serious scholarly studies were undertaken after the end of World War II. In the 1940's, most of the writings are of a general, narrative nature. John Bakeless, in his 1947 book, *Partners in Discovery*,[4] offers an overall description of the great adventure. He begins with the planning of the expedition, continues with the dramatic details of the exploration and ends by discussing the aftermath and results of the enterprise. His narrative tells the story of the expedition in a very thorough and clear manner. The author is deeply impressed by the explorers' achievements, though he considers Lewis to have often been rash and reckless in his judgments. Bakeless's book is considered one of the first satisfactory accounts of the Lewis and Clark Expedition[5] and provided a foundation for later scholars. It also reflects the confident, even triumphalist mood of the United States following World War II.

In the same year that Bakeless's book appeared, Jay Monaghan produced a lengthy essay entitled "Lewis and Clark." Monaghan begins his account when Lewis was a boy and Jefferson first had thoughts of a westering exploration. He approaches the story in an individualistic manner, attempting to give the reader the background of each participant, and to humanize them, so that the reader may better understand how and why the events took place. Monaghan tries to establish the view that Lewis may have been "born" for this adventure, that it was destiny: "He was also a seeker of knowledge like Jefferson himself."[6] His account differs from the previous ones, in that as well as retelling the story of the expedition, it touches on political motives, and gives significant credit to the other members of the Corps, stating that each played an important role and had a unique personality. In his analysis of the various personalities, he highlights the importance of the psychological interplay between the expedition's members. Monaghan even mentions York, Clark's Negro slave who went along on the difficult trip. York would become a subject of interest to future historians, as would Sacagawea, the Indian woman who played a role in the success of the expedition. Monaghan describes her participation as well. *Transition to next author*

By the 1950s, historians began to take a deeper look into not only the adventurous aspects of the expedition, but the impact that the exploration had on the development of the United States. Bernard De Voto, who also edited a selection of the Lewis and Clark journals,[7] published a book called *The Course of Empire* in 1952. Since De Voto's book is on western exploration generally, the Lewis and Clark Expedition forms only a part of his story, yet he devotes considerable space to it. Like previous historians, De Voto points out the romantic and adventurous aspects, noting that "one who spends time reading the records of wilderness men is in danger of taking for granted the labor, strain, hardship, weariness, hunger, thirst, passion, fear, anger, pain, desire and wonder that were their fare."[8] Yet De Voto also *Transition to next author*

Short quotation set off by a colon

stresses the importance of this expedition by connecting it to Jefferson's goal of establishing an empire of liberty: "Here was the Great South Sea, the Pacific Ocean and they had brought the United States to its shore."[9] With this, he implies the major impact that the expedition had on the future success of the United States. Most importantly, De Voto calls attention to the fact that many technical aspects of the Lewis and Clark Expedition had been neglected and needed further comprehensive study. This observation led to a richer historiography of the expedition, as writers began to look more into the achievements of the Corps of Discovery in the field of natural history.

Transition to next author

Responding to this perceived need for greater attention to the Corps' scientific achievements, Raymond Darwin Burroughs released his book, *The Natural History of the Lewis and Clark Expedition, in 1961*.[10] Burroughs approached the history in a very scientific manner. Following a brief narrative history of the expedition in the introduction, the rest of the book is quite technical. He divides the book into chapters that are named after the animals that were discovered and studied by Lewis and Clark during their journey, which included bears, raccoons, weasels, wild dogs and cats, and bison. Lewis and Clark are credited with being the first to give reliable descriptions of wildlife populations in this area. Throughout his book, Burroughs stresses the importance of the thorough analysis of the natural discoveries made by the expedition, and their impact on scientific study.

Transition to next author

Paul Russell Cutright, in his 1969 book, *Lewis and Clark: Pioneering Naturalists,* successfully accomplishes the goals set by both De Voto and Burroughs.[11] Like them, he calls attention to the neglect of the technical aspects of the Lewis and Clark Expedition among historians. Cutright offers what he believes is the reason for the neglect of the scientific aspects of the expedition, claiming that the slighting of the scientific phases had its inception almost immediately after Lewis and Clark concluded their historic journey. Thomas Jefferson, early in 1807, appointed Meriwether Lewis to the post of Governor of the Territory of Louisiana instead of allowing him to devote all his energies and talents to writing the narrative, including scientific discoveries of the expedition. It was an illusory reward and a consequential error, as Jefferson would soon learn. Cutright goes on to explain that Lewis died an unexpected death and that the volumes were edited by other writers who left out much of the natural history. Cutright, a biologist, meets his objectives by presenting a careful assessment of the expedition's scientific accomplishments. He focuses on botany, zoology, geography, anthropology, and medicine. His book contains many historical facts about the events and the people involved but these facts revolve around his main purpose of presenting to the reader the major scientific contributions made by Lewis and Clark. He concludes each chapter with a summary of the discoveries within each area traversed by the Corps.

Interest in the scientific aspects of the expedition did not end with Cutright, but rather continued with an even deeper focus. The often harrowing facts concerning the health of the expedition members seem almost fictional in nature. It is nothing short of a miracle that all but one of the original members survived the long and dangerous exploration of the Wild West. Several writers were intrigued by this fact and were compelled to study and write about it. Now the history of the Lewis and Clark Expedition would take on a medical perspective.

Transitional paragraph to works dealing with the medical history of the expedition

The medical aspects of the expedition came to the fore in a 1971 article entitled "Lewis and Clark: Westering Physicians."[12] The author, Drake Will, employs a narrative style but his story revolves strictly around the health, illnesses, and treatments of the exploring party. Will's introduction includes portions of a letter written by Thomas Jefferson to Dr. Benjamin Rush of Philadelphia, asking Doctor Rush to prepare some notes for Captain Lewis. His notes were to include several medical questions about the native people and some directions for the preservation of Lewis's health as well as the health of the other members of the Corps. Will goes into detail about the various illnesses experienced by the members and informs the reader about the remedies and treatments that were used by both Lewis and Clark throughout the journey. Interestingly, he even explains the medical events involved in the birth of Sacagawea's baby, Pompey. Nor did Will omit the fact that the men of the Corps purchased moments of passion from the native women and consequently contracted venereal diseases. Will also mentions the fact that Lewis and Clark were for the most part very skeptical of the medical practices of the native people, even though at times, they reported the apparent success of such practices.

Continuing the emphasis on the medical history of the Lewis and Clark Expedition was Eldon Chuinard, a medical doctor, in his 1979 book, *Only One Man Died*. It is not surprising that Dr. Chuinard would be fascinated by the fact that although a licensed physician did not accompany the Corps of Discovery on this dangerous expedition, only one man failed to survive. In the introduction, Dr. Chuinard *ellipses to show omitted material at end of sentence* mentions a comment made by Bernard DeVoto in his book, *The Course of Empire* to the effect that the medical aspects of the expedition had received little attention. To this comment Chuinard replies: "To this author this subject is interesting and important; and it has been my effort in this book to exhaust the subject without exhausting the reader. . . ."[13]

Dr. Chuinard states his objectives clearly in the introduction:

block quotation

> This book is not meant to be another general and complete review of the story of the Expedition. Terrain, climate, geography, biology, botany, and the commercial aspects are muted, being mentioned to orient the reader in time and place, and mainly for the purpose of indicating their effects on the health of the men. . . . only enough of the geography, climate, edibles and Indian customs are excerpted from the journals to indicate the health problems that the Expedition faced in certain locations and conditions. . . . therefore the scope of medical reference is considerably more extensive than the recounting of specific diseases and their treatments.[14]

The author writes about the medical practices of Lewis and Clark and credits them with considerable success in the treatment of the expedition's members. Dr. Chuinard believes that although the captains were not physicians by occupation, "they were truly great physicians in native ability and devotion."[15] Chuinard includes lists of medicines that were purchased for the journey. He describes the illnesses and treatments that were experienced by all the members, and devotes an entire chapter to Indian medicine. His amazement that the expedition accomplished all of the President's requests while losing only one man is evident throughout his book.

Yet another writer interested in the scientific aspects of the journey was the geographer John Logan Allen. In his 1979 book, *Passage through the Garden, Lewis and Clark and the Image of the American Northwest*, Allen examines the expedition's geographical achievements. After exhaustively analyzing every map, narrative, and scrap of information that the explorers had at the start of their journey, the author is able to present a clear picture of the explorers' mental image of the region. He then shows how their discoveries altered this image, and shattered many erroneous beliefs, such as that the Rockies were of the same height as the Appalachians. This profusely illustrated volume allows the reader to gain a much clearer sense of the changes brought about by the expedition in the field of geographic knowledge.[16]

Some historians have focused their attention not on the expedition as a whole, or on some aspect of it such as medical care, but rather on its two heroic leaders. This biographical approach to the topic can be seen in Richard Dillon's 1965 book, *Meriwether Lewis.* Dillon's main purpose in writing the biography was to consider Lewis in isolation from the expedition and especially from Clark, so that the reader might better understand the "one man who deserves to be considered as the person who opened up the Far West." Dillon seems adamant about persuading the reader away from thinking of Lewis as only half of a partnership with Clark, and is critical of the failure of previous writers and historians to focus on each of the expedition's leaders individually: "Both Lewis and Clark have suffered from this shotgun marriage of convenience, brokered by lazy historians more content with image than reality."[17] Dillon attempts a full reappraisal of Lewis, who, he argues, was much more important than Clark to the success of the expedition. Dillon calls attention to two characteristics of Lewis that, in his opinion, are often unnoticed. The first is Lewis's narrative abilities in the writing of his national epic. The second characteristic is Lewis's superior ability as a diplomat among the Indian nations.

Transition to discussion of works with a biographical focus

run-in quotation

The other half of the famous duo has not been ignored by biographers. In 1977, Jerome Steffen published his study of William Clark. The book, entitled *William Clark: Jeffersonian Man on the Frontier,* provides information about Clark's early years as well as his post-expedition accomplishments. Steffen suggests that Lewis may have been given more credit than he deserved in regard to the scientific success of the Corps of Discovery: "The expedition provided an intellectual opportunity for a man who, from boyhood, had demonstrated a deep interest in natural science and history. Clark made innumerable scientific contributions to the expedition, many usually attributed to his partner."[18] Unlike Dillon, Steffen is not anxious to study Clark in isolation from Lewis. His goal is to identify William Clark as an eighteenth century Enlightenment figure.

The historiography of the Lewis and Clark Expedition has been enriched by the perspectives of the histories of ethnic minorities that have developed over the last few decades. The complex relationship between the expedition and the native peoples they encountered was, until the 1960s, only lightly covered. In the earlier works discussed in this essay, the Indians were mentioned only in a general manner and for the purpose of glorifying the civilized ways of Lewis and Clark. In the medical aspects of the expedition's history, the Indians tend to be blamed for soldiers' venereal diseases.

Transition to works focusing on Native Americans

A deepening interest in the native people of the West emerges as early as 1966, when John Ewers published his article called "Plains Indian Reactions to the Lewis and Clark Expedition." For the first time, the history of the expedition was interpreted from a native perspective. Ewers explains that the encounter of these Indians with Lewis and Clark was by no means their first encounter with whites. By this time the Indians had been trading with them for quite some time. For the most part, Indians were suspicious of whites. They were not ignorant of the interest that white men had in them and in the resources of their country. Despite this, the overall reaction of the Indians to Lewis and Clark was fair. Ewers concentrates his study mostly on the Mandan Tribe. He does this because Lewis and Clark spent several months near the Mandan villages and these Indians had a greater opportunity to get to know the explorers. Ewers goes into detail about the relationship between the Mandan Indians and the explorers. For the most part, the Mandans regarded Lewis and Clark in a friendly manner, but the author concludes that in the field of diplomacy, the expedition was not as successful as in other fields. Ewers claims that the reactions of the Indians to Lewis and Clark were of historical importance: "The reactions of these Indians to their meetings with Lewis and Clark were important to the future relations of United States Citizens with the native peoples of an area larger than that of the original thirteen states."[19]

James R. Ronda continued the emphasis on the Indian encounters with the expedition. His book, *Lewis and Clark among the Indians,* was released in 1984. Ronda's purpose in writing the book was to shift the focus of the history of the expedition to the Indian-white encounters in North America. This approach is symptomatic of a tendency during the last two decades for historians, especially those writing on the history of the Americas, to dispense with the concept of heroic "discovery" by white men and recast it as a series of "encounters." Ronda makes clear, from the beginning, that his book is not another general review of the famous expedition. He concentrates on the daily dealings of the Indians with the Corps of Discovery and gives much detail about the customs and culture of the Indians: "In the simplest terms, this book is about what happens when people from different cultural persuasions meet and deal with each other."[20] He gives much credit to Lewis and Clark for the gathering of information on the natives which has helped historians to better understand the culture of the Indians during this period. Ronda credits himself with filling a gap in the history of the Lewis and Clark Expedition and for offering a fresh approach as well. He shares Ewers's view that, overall, the expedition failed in Indian diplomacy. Ronda makes a final statement about the important role that the Indians played in the success of the exploration. Furthermore, he points to the presence of Sacagawea in the group as a key to understanding just how important the support of the natives was to the survival of the explorers.

Even before Ronda's book appeared, historians had begun to look in detail at the intrepid Indian woman. Ella Clark and Margot Edmonds, in *Sacagawea of the Lewis and Clark Expedition* (1979), tackled the controversy over Sacagawea's true role in the enterprise. Popular but unfounded beliefs about the brave and beautiful Indian woman had her single-handedly guiding the large expedition through unexplored territory, and dying as an old woman in Wind River, Wyoming, in 1884. While demonstrating that neither of these beliefs is supported by the evidence, the authors do relate in considerable detail the significant contributions of Sacagawea to the expedition. Their biography is an attempt to clarify the truth about the "myths," as they call them:

> It is the aim of this biography to place Sacagawea's life and accomplishments in historical perspective, and to dispel the fog of idolatry which has surrounded her for so long. Our intention is not, as might be supposed, to depreciate what she did or to lessen her role in the Lewis and Clark Expedition. On the contrary, we hope to emphasize her importance by plainly stating the part she played in a historic feat.[21]

block quotation

The first part of the book tells the story of Sacagawea's role in the Lewis and Clark Expedition, while the second part covers her life following the expedition. It seems natural that Sacagawea would become a focus of attention for historians in the 1970s, at a time when the fight for women's equality and recognition was prominent, and women's history had emerged as a significant area of study.

Another member of the expedition whose role was in need of clarification was William Clark's slave, York. The attention paid to York is certainly connected to the emergence of African American history as an important field during the last few decades. Robert B. Betts makes an attempt at this clarification in his 1985 book, *In Search of*

Transition to work on African American member of expedition

York. As with Sacagawea, it was York's fate that many myths were created about his role in the expedition. He has been portrayed as a tall, strong man who contributed only entertainment in the form of comedy, to the rest of the Corps, and who had an amicable slave relationship with his master. Betts boldly claims: "How this came about is in itself a cameo example of the way our history was for so long presented from an almost exclusively white point of view. . . ." He continues by stating the primary purpose of his book, which is "to break through the stereotype and try to see York as a credible human being, a man who knew firsthand his country at its best and its worst—from the heights of magnificent achievement of the exploration to the depths of slavery."[22] Betts accomplishes his goal by offering details about York and his participation in the expedition. He obtained most of this information directly from what was written about York in the journals. Betts makes no secret about his disappointment in the failure of historians, both black and white, to take seriously this forgotten slave, who in Betts's opinion, made important contributions to the expedition.

run-in quotation

Several works on the expedition published during the 1990s, partly under the influence of postmodernist interest in deconstructing historical "discourses," focus on the language employed by members of the Corps in their letters and journals. Albert Furtwangler examines the Lewis and Clark Expedition as history, literature, and science, in his book, *Acts of Discovery: Visions of America in the Lewis and Clark Journals,* published in 1993.[23] Furtwangler, a specialist in American literature, argues that the journals are not simply primary source materials for historians, but should also be considered an important literary work. He is more interested in the idea of discovery, and how this idea evolved in the minds of Lewis and Clark during their journey, than he is in the external events of the discovery. The author is especially concerned with how Lewis and Clark fashioned new modes of expression to convey their encounters with new terrain, people, animals, plants, and foods.

Transition to recent works, some of them post- modernist, dealing with the writings of the expedition

In 1994, Gunther Barth examined the impact of the expedition's journals in his article, "Timeless Journals: Reading Lewis and Clark With Nicholas Biddle's Help." Barth reviews the publication history of the journals of the expedition, focusing in on the contributions of Nicholas Biddle, who was the author of *History of the Expedition of Captains Lewis and Clark,* published in 1814. He begins with an overview of the expedition and notes that Biddle, not Lewis or Clark, was the main source of knowledge about the enterprise through the nineteenth century. Biddle chose to downplay any elements of doubt or confusion in the captains' behavior, and to ignore all references in the journals to topics like sex and venereal disease. The resulting expurgated and sanitized journals, according to Barth, presented a grand, heroic narrative that suited the nationalistic needs of nineteenth century Americans, and changed its leaders into "taciturn classic heroes."[24] Continuing this interest in closely analyzing the language of the explorers, Frank Bergon published an article in 1997 titled "Wilderness Aesthetics." Bergon praises Lewis and Clark for their "fresh, flexible, uses of the vernacular" that anticipate writers like Thoreau, but his overall assessment is critical: "In portending the destruction of one civilization and the rise of another, the journals reveal the dark, imperialistic underside of the epical adventure."[25]

Combination of run-in quotation with one set off by a colon

The most recent among the books discussed here is also the most impressive: Stephen E. Ambrose's *Undaunted Courage: Meriwether Lewis, Thomas Jefferson, and the Opening of the American West* (1996). A comprehensive account of the background and details of the expedition, Ambrose's book resembles some of the much earlier works in its celebration of courage. The author examines Lewis's close and enduring friendship with Thomas Jefferson, and shows how faithfully Lewis reflected the President's passionate interest in the commercial potential as well as the scientific discoveries of the expedition. The overall tone is adulatory, and Ambrose does not accept Bakeless's negative assessment of Lewis. He does admit that Lewis mishandled several crises in the wilderness, but considers these occasional and uncharacteristic lapses of judgment. Putting these missteps into context with Lewis's alcohol problem, and his suicide several years later, Ambrose suggests that he was probably manic depressive.[26] The author takes fully into account the recent, more specialized scholarship on the expedition, making this highly readable book a skilful work of synthesis as well as a careful study based on primary source materials.

Over the years since Meriwether Lewis and William Clark led the Corps of Discovery across the uncharted wilderness to the Pacific Ocean and back, its achievements and significance for America have been carefully studied. The earlier emphasis on the journey as an epic of courage and heroism has, through the years, evolved historiographically into more tightly focused analyses and interpretations, involving such topics as natural discoveries, medical aspects, geography, and perspectives based on the history of Native Americans, women, and blacks. The recent postmodernist interest in deconstructing historical narratives has also attracted scholars to the topic. Scholarly interest in the Lewis and Clark Expedition shows no sign of fading. Rather, it is likely to increase with the approach of the bicentennial of the expedition, and with the release of the final

concluding paragraph notes the overall evolution of the historiography and anticipates future interest in the topic

volumes of the most complete and accurate scholarly edition of the Lewis and Clark Journals ever published.[27]

Endnotes

1. An example of the eccentric spelling employed by both Lewis and Clark.

2. Quoted in Stephen E. Ambrose, *Undaunted Courage: Meriwether Lewis, Thomas Jefferson, and the Opening of the American West* (New York: Simon and Schuster, 1996), 310.

3. Actually, only Lewis held the rank of captain. Clark was still a lieutenant. However, Lewis insisted that they were co-commanders, and the enlisted men, believing them to be of equal rank, addressed them both as "Captain." Ambrose, 134–6.

4. John Bakeless, *Lewis and Clark: Partners in Discovery* (New York: William Morrow & Company, 1947).

5. According to *Readers Guide to American History* (Boston: Houghton Mifflin, 1991), 402.

6. Jay Monaghan, "Lewis and Clark," in *Overland Trail* (Indianapolis: Bobbs-Merrill Co., 1947), 34.

7. Bernard De Voto, ed., *The Journals of Lewis and Clark* (Boston: Houghton, Mifflin, 1953).

8. Bernard DeVoto, *The Course of Empire* (Boston: Houghton, Mifflin, 1952), xvii.

9. DeVoto, *The Course of Empire,* 553.

10. Raymond Darwin Burroughs, *The Natural History of the Lewis and Clark Expedition* (East Lansing: Michigan State University Press, 1961).

11. Paul Russell Cutright, *Lewis and Clark: Pioneering Naturalists* (Urbana: University of Illinois Press, 1969).

12. Drake Will, "Westering Physicians," *Montana History* 21 (Autumn 1971): 2–17.

13. Eldon Chuniard, *Only One Man Died: The Medical Aspects of the Lewis and Clark Expedition* (Glendale: Arthur H. Clark Company, 1979), 26.

14. Chuinard, 27–28.

15. Chuinard, 31.

16. John Logan Allen, *Passage through the Garden: Lewis and Clark and the Image of the American Northwest* (Urbana: University of Illinois Press, 1975).

17. Richard Dillon, *Meriwether Lewis: A Biography* (New York: Coward-McCann, 1965), xiii.

18. Jerome Steffen, *William Clark: Jeffersonian Man on the Frontier* (Norman: University of Oklahoma Press, 1977), 6.

19. John Ewers, "Plains Indian Reactions to the Lewis and Clark Expedition," *Montana History* 16 (Winter 1966): 2.

20. James P. Ronda, *Lewis and Clark among the Indians* (Lincoln: University of Nebraska Press, 1984), xi.

21. Ella Clark and Margot Edmonds, *Sacagawea of the Lewis and Clark Expedition* (Berkeley: University of California Press, 1979), 2.

22. Robert B. Betts, *In Search of York* (Boulder: Colorado Associated University Press, 1985), 6.

23. Albert Furtwangler, *Acts of Discovery, Visions of America in the Lewis and Clark Journals.* (Urbana: University of Illinois Press, 1993).

24. Gunther Barth, "Timeless Journals: Reading Lewis and Clark with Nicholas Biddle's Help," *Pacific Historical Review* 63 (1994): 515.

25. Frank Bergon, "Wilderness Aesthetics," *American Literary History* 9 (1997): 133, 159.

26. Ambrose, 312.

27. Gary E. Moulton, ed., *The Journals of the Lewis and Clark Expedition,* 13 vols. (Lincoln: University of Nebraska Press, 1983–). The final volumes of this edition are scheduled to be published by 2003.

Bibliography

Allen, John Logan. *Passage through the Garden: Lewis and Clark and the Image of the American Northwest.* Urbana: University of Illinois Press, 1975.

Ambrose, Stephen E. *Undaunted Courage: Meriwether Lewis, Thomas Jefferson, and the Opening of the American West.* New York: Simon and Schuster, 1996.

Barth, Gunther. "Timeless Journals: Reading Lewis and Clark with Nicholas Biddle's Help." *Pacific Historical Review* 63 (1994): 499–519.

Bakeless, John. *Lewis and Clark: Partners in Discovery.* New York: William Morrow and Company, 1947.

Bergon, Frank. "Wilderness Aesthetics." *American Literary History* 9 (1997): 128–61.

Betts, Robert. *In Search of York.* Boulder: Colorado Associated University Press, 1985.

Burroughs, Raymond Darwin. *The Natural History of the Lewis and Clark Expedition.* East Lansing: Michigan State University Press, 1961.

Chuinard, Eldon G. *Only One Man Died: The Medical Aspects of the Lewis and Clark Expedition.* Glendale: The Arthur H. Clark Company, 1979.

Clark, Ella, and Margot Edmonds. *Sacagawea of the Lewis and Clark Expedition.* Berkeley: University of California Press, 1979.

Cutright, Paul Russell. *Lewis and Clark: Pioneering Naturalists.* Urbana: University of Illinois Press, 1969.

DeVoto, Bernard. *The Course of Empire.* Boston: Houghton, Mifflin, 1952.

Dillon, Richard. *Meriwether Lewis: A Biography.* New York: Coward-McCann, 1965.

Ewers, John. "Plains Indian Reactions to the Lewis and Clark Expedition." *Montana History* 16 (1966): 2–12.

Furtwangler, Albert. *Acts of Discovery, Visions of America*. Urbana: University of Illinois Press, 1993.

Monaghan, Jay. "Lewis and Clark." In *Overland Trail*. Indianapolis: Bobbs-Merrill Co., 1947.

Ronda, James R. *Lewis and Clark Among the Indians*. Lincoln: University of Nebraska Press, 1984.

Steffen, Jerome O. *William Clark: Jeffersonian Man on the Frontier*. Norman: University of Oklahoma Press, 1977.

Will, Drake. "Westering Physicians." *Montana History* 21 (1971): 2–17.

It will be noted that the concluding paragraph sums up the major approaches that have been taken by historians of this topic since the end of World War II. It also reminds the reader of the approaching bicentennial and suggests that considerable scholarly activity on this topic should be expected in the next few years. Endnotes rather than footnotes have been used. If the specifications for the paper had called for footnotes, these would have been placed at the bottom of each page (this is done automatically by selecting "footnotes" rather than "endnotes" in your word processor). Arabic numerals are used for notes. If the footnote/endnote menu on your word processor happens to be set to Roman numerals, change the setting to Arabic numerals. The bibliography, which comes last, should start on a separate page. Also, every page of the essay, including the bibliography, should be consecutively paginated, using the pagination function of your word processor. It is customary to leave the first page of text unpaginated. An unpaginated cover sheet should also be attached, giving the title of the paper, your name, course information, instructor, and date.

Alternative Approaches

Because we considered Ms. Autran's essay as a good example, it should not be imagined that the structure and style of all historiographic essays must conform to it. There are other successful methods of writing this kind of essay. It will be noted that in our example the author chose to organize the material chronologically—that is, proceeding from the first book discussed (published in 1947), through succeeding years up to the late 1990s. Alternatively, she might have employed a topical approach, in which, for example, all biographical works, or those concerned with the scientific activities of the expedition, were discussed in succession, regardless of their date of publication. The chronological approach usually works out best, but there is no rigid formula. Whether the approach is topical, chronological, or some combination thereof depends on many factors, not the least of which is simply the author's preference.

Regardless of the approach you choose to take, a number of valuable insights should emerge from the writing of a historiographic essay. For one thing, it is an especially valuable device for developing and honing your library research skills. Even more important, it encourages, indeed compels, the reading of history with an eye to understanding the approaches and methods of various historians. It enables you to think historiographically, an essential attainment for those who are serious about understanding history as an intellectual discipline. It also puts one in an excellent frame of mind for undertaking a major research paper, which we will examine next.

CHAPTER FIVE

Engaging with Primary Sources: The Research Paper

In the last chapter, we examined some effective methods of researching and writing the historiographic essay; in this chapter we will consider the same process for the research paper. The former is concerned almost entirely with secondary sources, while in the latter all available primary sources, as well as the relevant secondary works, are used. Moreover, a research paper is usually lengthier than a historiographic essay. A typical form in which the undergraduate encounters it is in the senior thesis—an extensive project sometimes extending over an entire academic year, often under the auspices of a seminar. A term paper in an upper-division history course may sometimes be extensive enough to qualify as a research paper, although usually it is shorter and based on relatively few sources. Still, many of the skills and methods requisite for the longer project will be quite applicable to the term paper as well.

A senior thesis or similar extensive research project can be considered a "capstone" experience of an undergraduate major in history. It brings together the knowledge and insights gained from previous courses, recently acquired research skills, and one's growing powers of analysis, imagination, and expression. It offers the opportunity to move beyond a somewhat passive mode of learning into the critical and analytical mode of the self-directed research scholar. Approached with the proper attitude of adventure and determination, it can prove to be the most valuable and memorable academic experience of one's undergraduate career.

SEARCHING FOR A VIABLE TOPIC

When setting out to write a research paper, it is important to have a topic of manageable scope, and, as with the historiographic essay, this will almost certainly entail some pruning of the subject you originally select. There are also considerations that are peculiar to the research paper. For example, it is usually necessary to choose a topic for which a significant quantity of primary source material is accessible to you. By checking on the availability of published sources (or even close-at-hand manuscripts that you know you are allowed to use) early in the research process, a potentially large waste of time can be averted. Otherwise, diligent research in the library catalog and various indexes might yield an admirable array of secondary works but few if any primary sources. It is possible, of course, that the nature of the topic or your instructor's guidelines might render a paucity of primary sources acceptable, but be sure to check.

At this point one might object that I have drawn too tight a distinction between primary and secondary sources. Is it not the case that the authors of books, articles, and essays often quote freely from primary materials? And, in writing a research paper, is it not perfectly acceptable to use and even quote the sources used by other historians? After all, the amount of primary source material that could be culled in this fashion from a couple of dozen secondary works might be considerable. The answer is that while it is acceptable to quote material quoted by others, it should be done sparingly and is not a substitute for reading through and selecting from a much larger mass of primary materials.

The rule is always to use the fullest, best-edited collection of any primary source available to you. Under this rule, the most "nutritious" source would be the unedited manuscripts or editions of these sources in which the manuscripts are reproduced in their entirety. From that state there is a descending scale in which more and more highly processed sources are used (as in *The Selected Letters of . . .*). Primary source material quoted in a secondary work is usually only a fraction of the body of material from which it was selected. In dealing with primary sources, the historian's task is to select representative and illustrative documents from as large a collection as possible. Becoming a sensitive, skillful, and efficient analyst of source material is a vital part of training to be a historian.

FINDING PRIMARY SOURCES

Since we explored the process of finding secondary works in the last two chapters, we can concentrate here on the process of locating primary sources. One method that was mentioned earlier, for finding collections of documents in book form, is to look under the various subject headings for your topic in the library catalog to see if there are any with the word "sources" added. If you are working on a biographical topic, or if your topic has significant biographical components, look for the name(s) of the major person(s) in your historical account under both Author *and* Subject entries. A Keyword search on a person should lead you to both. Anything written by any of your historical players is a primary source.

Another effective method is to look for published bibliographies on your topic, which may be in the form of essays or articles as well as books. Some of the major places to find the titles of published bibliographies are the subject heading catalog and the *Guide to Reference Books* edited by Balay (see Chapter Three). Many published bibliographies that you locate by any of these means will have a section on primary sources. Most will have a much larger chronological or topical sweep than your topic, and you will need to look up your time period or topic in the table of contents or index. A good example is *The Harvard Guide to American History,* an excellent reference source for primary and secondary sources, though it is a bit dated for the latter.[1] If you are working on some aspect of the American Revolution, for example, looking under that section in the *Harvard Guide* will refer you to several useful collections of published documents. You may also wish to investigate the availability of local manuscript sources and whether or not your library has an oral history collection.

In searching for published collections of primary sources, consult the bibliographies and footnotes of your secondary sources, as well as doing some creative shelf browsing. In many historical monographs, the bibliographies at the end of the book are divided into primary and secondary sources. The former is sometimes further subdivided into manuscript and published sources. In articles and essays, be sure to mine the footnotes for references to published sources. As for shelf browsing, it can be quite effective with regard to primary sources, especially if you are in the stage of still searching for a topic. If, for example, you decided you would like to do a research paper on modern India but had not refined the topic beyond that, your scanning of the library stacks on the history of India might reveal the massive, multivolume *Collected Works of Mahatma Gandhi.* The availability of this source could serve to point you toward a manageable topic, one that would probably but not necessarily be biographical in nature.

Finally, if the period you are studying falls during the last century or so, you may want to research newspapers or periodicals contemporary with the events you are studying. *The Times* (London) and the *New York*

1 Revised edition, ed. Frank Freidel (Cambridge, Mass: Belknap Press, 1974). This, by the way, is another example of a "split footnote."

Times are widely available on microfilm, and your library's reference room should have the indexes that will allow you to access these newspapers for material on particular topics or persons. Many other newspapers are also available, both on microfilm and as bound volumes, but the indexes to them that do exist usually do not go back before the 1970s. This need not preclude the use of unindexed newspapers, for if you are looking for items about particular events for which you know the dates, you can search the newspapers published immediately following the events. In regard to magazine articles from the period you are investigating, *Poole's Index* and *the Reader's Guide to Periodical Literature* will open up the riches of nineteenth- and twentieth-century periodical publications of a more popular bent.

Approaching Your Reading

It is unnecessary, indeed inadvisable, to defer reading until you have accumulated your entire list of sources. As was noted in the last chapter, it is a good idea to begin reading something immediately so as to gain some command over the basic factual detail and to assist you in refining the scope of your topic. It is best to begin your reading with the secondary works, because without some factual grasp of the topic, you will not be able to analyze the primary sources effectively. Also, it is necessary to be aware of some of the historiographic dimensions of your subject before you finish reading. This entails following the kind of procedure discussed in the last chapter for a historiographic essay. When you have gained an understanding of the kinds of questions posed and approaches taken by other historians, you will be much more skillful in your own encounters with the primary sources.

By no means should it be thought that I am advising a "hands off" policy on primary materials until all the secondary works have been digested. To begin with, such stern counsel would be hypocritical, since I never observe it myself. On the contrary, whenever I undertake a new project I can hardly wait to get my hands on the primary sources. Moreover, it would not be a good idea to observe a rigid order of reading. When writing a research paper you will be involved in two processes: 1) extracting information from the secondary works as well as analyzing them historiographically; 2) reading through a variety of primary sources, both for information and for quotable material. These two processes, if not quite simultaneous, are at least interwoven. Thus while questions are fresh in your mind from reading another historian's account, it is a good time to plunge into the primary sources. Sudden, unexpected insights and connections can occur by varying your reading in this fashion.

Another advantage of making an early foray into the primary materials is that many of them are direct, vivid, and dramatic. Alternating them with books, articles, and essays by other historians is a refreshing change of pace and an excellent device for maintaining a high level of interest in your subject. The same thing should apply to your reading of secondary works. Do not feel that you must plod through one weighty tome cover to cover before you can start reading another. There is no reason why you should not be working on several books at the same time. The main thing is not to adopt an overly rigid methodology. It is important to keep a fresh, lively attitude and to enjoy the process. Experiment with different ways of doing your reading until you find one that works best for you.

Notetaking

As you read, always have a stack of 5 x 8 or 4 x 6 notecards or your computer next to you. Lined index cards are not essential—pads of paper of this size work quite well. (The 3 x 5 cards used for bibliographies are too small for effective notetaking.) Many students and not a few scholars prefer to take research notes in spiral notebooks, but these have a number of drawbacks. Notes kept in this fashion (on consecutive pages) might work well enough for the relatively few sources consulted in a typical term paper, but this tends to prove restrictive and inefficient for larger projects, in all but the most expert hands. The major drawback is the lack of flexibility. With a notebook, you will not be able to group and regroup notes relating to the same subtopic. When the time arrives to write a particular portion of your paper, a very frustrating search through the notebook would be required. The same problem can apply to notetaking on your computer, unless you establish a good indexing system or use software designed for the purpose.

Notecards, on the other hand, can be quickly and easily segregated into stacks based on the facet of the subject to which they refer. Even if you divided your notebook into sections for each subtopic, it would still be inflexible, for it frequently happens that after the research for a project is completed, you decide to divide the subject into a quite different set of subtopics than you originally planned. If all your notes are in a notebook, you will be confronted with the problem of turning wildly back and forth to find notes on each of your new subtopics. With cards, it is supremely easy—you simply reshuffle them to correspond to your new subtopics or ideas. Also, you can rearrange the sequence of cards relating to each subtopic to reflect the sequence of points you plan to make in your paper. Another advantage is that a quick glance at the size of each stack of cards can indicate whether you need more material on a certain subtopic, should merge it with another, further subdivide it, or perhaps drop it all together.

Cards should be kept in some kind of file box, preferably with tabbed file separators dividing the cards for each subtopic. It is also a good idea to place some kind of identifying word or mark on the top line of each card, to facilitate filing after a notetaking session. Also, if all your cards have subtopic headings, they can be quickly resegregated should they ever be dropped or scattered. Beyond this minimal identifying mark (which might be simply a letter or a number) there should be a brief description on the first line, allowing you to tell the contents at a glance without having to read it all. This will save a good deal of time when you start writing or if you decide to rearrange the cards due to a change from your original plan.

Having considered the mechanics of notetaking, let us turn to the substance of the process. Students are often baffled as to how many and what types of notes they should take. Should you record each and every "fact" you read? If so, your stack of notecards would swell to unmanageable proportions before you finished reading the first book, and you would doubtless begin to experience writer's cramp, if not total burnout. You will encounter a tremendous amount of factual detail about your topic in your reading, most of which does not warrant the time and effort for a note. In the course of reading a large number of historians' accounts as well as primary sources you will acquire a familiarity with the major events, processes, and persons that constitute your subject. Take notes only on those facts that you have reason to think will be necessary in your later analysis of the subject and the writing of the paper. On the other hand, being too sparing in your notetaking will leave you with a paucity of material when the time to write arrives. Obviously it is a question of acquiring a sense of balance, something that comes with practice.

Putting certain facts on cards for later retrieval and analysis is only one of the purposes of notetaking. Another is to record the views of other historians regarding your topic. These might be described as historiographic notes. Remember that in the research paper you will not only illuminate your topic by the use of primary sources, but should also explain to your readers, at least to some extent, the historiographic dimensions of the topic. Another purpose is to record those primary sources, or some portion of them, that you think you may want to quote or cite in your paper.

Finally, you should take notes of your own thoughts and reflections as you read. This is part of the creative process in research. Perhaps some comparison suddenly occurs to you, or you think of a particular way that you would like to analyze certain documents when you get around to writing the paper. Do not count on remembering these insights later. Write them down, either on separate cards or as bracketed inserts on the cards containing notes on the material in question. It is also an excellent idea to keep a separate small notebook for the purpose of recording your more general, overarching ruminations, and to make notes to yourself about things to be researched, verified, or further explored later.

At this point perhaps it is best to illustrate the process of notetaking by quoting a note of my own. The project in question was research for a book on John Richard Green, who, you may recall from Chapter One, was the author of the very influential *Short History of the English People* (1874). In that part of my research dealing with the impact of the *Short History*, I came across an article written just after Green's death by a scholar who had worked with Green during the latter's tenure as a Church of England clergyman. I was struck by one passage and filled out the following notecard:

> Popularity of Short History
> "When men leaving Oxford wished to improve their minds,
> if they were rich they traveled, and if they were poor they
> read Green's Short History."
> —Philip Lyttleton Gell, "John Richard Green,"
> Contemporary Review 39 (1883): 738.

Several points should be observed about this notecard. Since it was written by a contemporary and friend of Green's, it is a quotation from a primary source. In fact, it is from an obituary article on Green. I took down the quote partly because it had a nice ring to it and was "atmospheric," that is, it nicely conveyed the tone and style of the Victorian intellectual circles in which Green moved. The card's heading tells me at a glance what the card is about and allows it to be filed with other cards on the same subtopic. I also took care to cite the source and page number for this quotation. My actual card has only the notation "Gell (1883), 738" since I already had a bibliography card for this article with a complete citation. Note, however, that I also included the date (1883) in this citation, allowing this source to be distinguished from any other works by the same author that might be in my bibliography. To be on the safe side, it would be a good idea to add a short title to distinguish this source from other works by Gell, in case he had published two or more in 1883.

It is also quite a short note, and it might be thought that the vacant space on the card could be used for other notes. This, however, would violate a cardinal principle of notetaking: only one fact, thought, idea, or quotation per card. To do otherwise is to undermine the flexibility of the card system. The final thing that should be said about this card is that I did not end up using it. When I got around to writing the book,[2] I decided, somewhat reluctantly, to omit it. The focus of the chapter in which I had planned to use the quotation had changed from my original intent, and now the quote seemed peripheral and unnecessary. You will almost certainly take a good many more notes than you actually use in the writing of the paper, but this is inherent in the scholarly process. A thoughtful, judicious selection of material from your reading should be followed by a thoughtful, judicious selection from your own notes when it comes time to write.

THE OUTLINE AND STRUCTURE OF YOUR PAPER

Well before you are finished your research and are ready to write, you should begin developing an outline of your paper. It is important to give this matter some thought even at the start of your research. Although any outline you come up with at this point will necessarily be tentative and undeveloped, it will nonetheless launch you into the process of thinking structurally and help you to direct your research efficiently. As with all papers, the major divisions of the research paper are the introduction, the body of the paper, and the conclusion. It is with the outline of the body of the paper that you should chiefly concern yourself. Initially you will simply be blocking in a few major topics, but as you continue to read, think, and take notes, your outline will develop accordingly. Your outline should in fact continue to be amended even as you enter the writing phase. One of the most counterproductive postures you can adopt is to imagine that your outline is at some stage chiseled on stone tablets. You must be free at any time throughout the process to adopt changes, sometimes of major proportions.

2 Anthony Brundage, *The People's Historian: John Richard Green and the Writing of History in Victorian England* (Westport, Conn.: Greenwood Press, 1994).

The fully developed outline is the blueprint for the sequence of paragraphs that will constitute your paper. Just as the various topics and subtopics in the outline are related to paragraphs and clusters of paragraphs in the paper, they are also related to the notecards you are filling out, arranging, and classifying. Your notecards, in fact, are an important key to developing an effective outline. When each notecard is filled out, there is a brief entry on the top line describing the contents. When cards dealing with the same thing are aggregated, they provide one of your topics or subtopics. The number of notes in each group will tell you how much material you have on each subtopic and suggest to you if further subdivision is needed. It may be that you have only a few notes on a particular subtopic, which presents you with a decision about whether to do additional research in that area, merge that subtopic with another, or perhaps to drop it altogether. Each time this happens, you should amend your outline accordingly.

A recognition of the interrelationship between your clusters of notes and the items on the outline will help you keep some sense of balance and symmetry to your project. But an outline does not simply reflect the noted material you have accumulated. It should also be a sequence of topics and subtopics, each one of which leads smoothly into the next. That is, your outline establishes a structure for the natural and graceful set of linkages that the completed paper should exhibit. A careful look at your evolving outline can alert you to harsh disjunctions and allow you to rearrange sequences to permit an easy transition from one topic to another.

SOME ELEMENTS OF EFFECTIVE WRITING

"Always start at the beginning" may not be the best advice to offer someone engaged in a research paper. In many cases, the introduction is best left in a relatively incomplete state until the body of the paper, and possibly even the conclusion, is completed. As we have seen, it is very likely that the focus of the topic will shift somewhat, not only during the research phase but even during the writing. Nonetheless, a couple of functions of a good introduction should be noted. First, it should clearly inform the reader about the nature and scope of the paper. It should also include something on the basic historiographic dimensions of the subject, along with an indication of the approach you are taking. Another important function of a good introduction is to engage the reader's interest. Clarity is always an excellent means to this end. Some writers start with a vivid passage describing a central event or process, in order to create atmosphere and draw the reader into the topic, before going on to describing the scope of the paper. This is not appropriate in all cases, but for many topics such a "hook" can provide an effective beginning.

An impressive use of this device can be seen in the opening paragraphs of *The Crucial Decade*, the late Eric F. Goldman's classic study of the United States following World War II. Consider how powerfully the author creates the atmosphere of 1945 in a few deft narrative paragraphs:

> A U.S. Radio monitor in a little frame house in Oregon caught the first hint. The Japanese were interested in peace, the Domei broadcast said, provided that the prerogatives of the Emperor would not be "prejudiced." Then came two days of diplomacy, a few hours of false armistice, more waiting through an interminable weekend. Finally, on Tuesday, August 14, 1945, reporters were summoned to the Oval Office of the White House. President Truman glanced at the clock to make sure he was holding to the agreement of simultaneous announcement in Washington, London, and Moscow. At exactly 7 P.M. he began reading: Late that afternoon a message had been received from the Japanese Government which "I deem . . . full acceptance of . . . unconditional surrender."
>
> Across America the traditional signs of victory flared and thousands snakedanced in a pouring rain and a St. Louis crowd, suddenly hushing its whistles and tossing aside the confetti, persuaded a minister to hold services at 2 A.M. New York City, hardly unaccustomed to furor, amazed itself. With the first flash of V-J, up went the windows and down came the torn telephone books, the hats, bottles, bolts of silk, books, wastebaskets, and shoes, more than five thousand tons of jubilant litter. Whole families made their way to Times Square until two million people were milling about, breaking into snatches of the conga, hugging and kissing anybody in sight, greeting each twinkle of V-J news on the Times electric sign with a cheer that roared from the East River to the Hudson. The hoopla swirled on into the dawn, died down, broke out again the next afternoon, finally subsided only with another midnight.
>
> Americans had quite a celebration and yet, in a way, the celebration never really rang true. People were so gay, so determinedly gay. The nation was a carnival but the festivities, as a reporter wrote from Chicago, "didn't seem like so much. It was such a peculiar peace. . . . And everybody talked of 'the end of the war,' not of 'victory.'" The President himself spoke with a mixed tone. When the crowds around the White House chanted: "We want Harry," he appeared beaming with Bess on his arm and proclaimed this "a great day." His face quickly sobered as he added warnings of an "emergency ahead—a crisis as great . . . as December 7, 1941." At V-J, 1945, the United States was entering the newest of its eras in a curious, unprecedented jumble of moods.[3]

3 Eric F. Goldman, *The Crucial Decade and After: America, 1945–1960* (New York: Vintage Books, 1961), 3–4.

Goldman not only gives us vivid narrative here, he also delineates the atmosphere of 1945 and hints at its complexity. Criticisms of this type of approach as being too "popular" or "journalistic" are sometimes made. In response, it might be said that among the various possible reactions to reading Goldman's introductory paragraphs, closing the book seems the least likely.

Acquiring and maintaining a reader's interest should be a high priority for all historians, not just in the introduction but throughout the work. It is true, of course, that many topics do not readily lend themselves to the kind of anecdotal treatment just described. It is also true that telling a story well is only a part of the historian's calling. Imposing pattern and meaning on a jumble of events is the historian's central task. This often requires a tone of dispassionate analysis, and the use of generalization and abstraction rather than the relating of an exciting narrative. Obviously, any portion of your work can either be well written or poorly written. While your readers should not expect to be kept "entertained" all the time, they do have the right to as much incisiveness, clarity, and wit as you can at all times muster.

Attention to mechanics (like an effective outline) has an obviously beneficial effect on your written work. A clear, straightforward structure in which each section is designed to lead naturally into the next is essential. Things are not quite so clear when it comes to effective style. Here we are dealing with matters such as syntax and word choice, in which many different "correct" choices are possible. Furthermore, writing style is, or should be, as distinctive as personality. One way your writing is sure to undergo improvement, however, is through the active and critical reading of many well-written histories. By taking care to note how other authors structure their works and deploy language effectively, you can gain insights into your own writing.

There are, of course, some frequently cited injunctions, such as avoiding the use of long, convoluted sentences or short, choppy ones, and especially a long succession of sentences of the same length. Such admonitions, however, are qualified. The judicious use of the complex or very brief sentence enlivens your writing and is a relief to the eye and ear. All stylistic "rules" are only general guidelines, which the confident writer will not hesitate to ignore when the occasion demands. There are some sound practices that enhance word choice, such as a ready resort to the dictionary and thesaurus. One of the major ways to improve writing style is being willing to undertake multiple revisions of your work. It is often said that "writing is rewriting." Whatever the level of your expressive abilities and the facility with which you write, there is no substitute for careful editing and reworking, a process we will consider in more detail later in the chapter.

AN OPEN MIND AND INTELLECTUAL HONESTY

Apart from effective structure and style, concerns shared equally by writers in all subjects, there is an issue with which historians at any level should be especially concerned: intellectual honesty. I am not suggesting that there is any widespread problem of historians consciously setting out to deceive their readers or distort the truth. I am talking about making a determined effort to be genuinely impartial in selecting, analyzing, and presenting evidence. Most of us like to think of ourselves as impartial and fair minded, but deploying this attitude to good effect in research and writing is not as simple as it sounds. Even if a topic is new to us, we usually start with some slight knowledge of it and some interpretation of it, however hazy and unformed. This, indeed, is a good starting point. At an early stage of your research, ask yourself such questions as: What do I know about this subject and what do I consider its significance? What views do I have about the motives of the major decisionmakers involved? What impact did the events and people I will be dealing with have on subsequent history? Jot these questions down, and return to them periodically as a method of guarding against the unconscious tendency of looking for and seeing only that evidence that bolsters your preconceptions. As you research and reflect, consider as many alternative answers to your questions as possible.

Just as we must guard against partiality in selecting evidence, the same care must be taken in analyzing it. Primary sources need to be treated with respect as well as skepticism. If, like a trial lawyer or a debater, you proceed as though you are involved in an adversarial format, you will end up amassing only that evidence favorable to your side, and then torturing its meaning to fit a desired outcome. Remaining open-minded is crucial to being an effective researcher; it also helps ensure that your ideas and your work will develop in exciting and unanticipated ways. This is not to say that historians should avoid assertiveness in their interpretation of events or refrain from debates with other scholars. As we have seen, it is precisely these characteristics that make history the lively, dynamic, and valuable discipline it is. What is crucial is that our firmly held convictions be the result of our scholarly labors and not a set of prejudices resolutely fortified by turning a blind eye to contrary or even unpleasant evidence.

QUOTING

As was mentioned, one commonly observed characteristic of student research papers is that they are too heavily laden with quotes. There are no doubt many reasons why student authors tend to bolster their work with the words of others. The least charitable explanation is that it seems an expeditious way of filling the requisite number of pages for the paper, but I doubt that this accounts for more than a handful of cases. More common is the notion that generous chunks of primary source material will, in addition to functioning as evidence, impart atmosphere to the paper. This is sometimes the case, but only if the material is evocative, well stated, and appropriate. Even then, the rule should be to quote only as much of a passage as is necessary without destroying or distorting the meaning of the longer document from which it is excerpted. Otherwise, you should simply describe or paraphrase the contents of the document. Overly lengthy or ill-chosen quotations impede the text and weary the reader. Quotations should never be allowed to become roadblocks in the smooth flow of historical narrative and analysis.

With these caveats in mind, let us consider some of the mechanics of quotation. When you find a passage you think you might like to use in your paper, fill out a notecard, or make a computer entry, indicating the precise reference to the source. If you are uncertain just how much of the quote you will be using, play it safe and note an extended passage. You can decide later about how much of it to insert into your paper. Often, you will find that there are various portions of a document you want to use, separated by material that is extraneous to your purpose. In this case, you can omit the unwanted material provided that: a) by your omission you do not distort the meaning of the passage or the context in which it appears; b) you indicate that material has been omitted by the use of ellipsis points.

Examples of the use of ellipsis points (or ellipses)—three evenly spaced periods—are to be seen in the introductory paragraphs of Eric Goldman's *The Crucial Decade*, quoted above. When Goldman tells of President Truman's announcement of the Japanese surrender, he quotes only one sentence and prunes it considerably so that it flows into his narrative: Late that afternoon a message had been received from the Japanese Government which "I deem . . . full acceptance of . . . unconditional surrender." A couple of paragraphs later, Goldman again uses ellipses to good effect in quoting the words of a Chicago reporter: "It was such a peculiar peace. . . . And everybody talked of 'the end of the war,' not of 'victory.'"

In the first passage the omitted material, indicated by the two sets of ellipsis points, is within a single sentence. In the second passage we know the omitted material is more than one sentence because there is a period immediately after the word "peace" and before the ellipsis points. Note also that the word "And" is capitalized, indicating that in the original source it is the beginning of another sentence. Did Goldman meet the other requirement of the use of ellipsis points, namely that the omission of material not distort the meaning of the document? Only a check of the full sources he used can answer that question. But it easy to see how very distorted the meaning of the original would have been had the author left out the final phrase of the Chicago reporter's second sentence, so that it read: "And everybody talked of 'the end of the war'. . . ." This is an accurate quote, and ellipsis points are used, but eliminating the phrase "not of 'victory'" utterly confounds and obscures the original meaning.

Ellipsis points are a most helpful device, allowing the use of only those portions of a document that are of interest to you. They permit a very flexible tailoring of quoted material so that it meshes with your writing without impeding the narrative flow. This smooth integration of primary material with your work is easiest when the material quoted is brief-a sentence or less. There are times, of course, when you need to quote lengthier passages, perhaps as much as a paragraph or so. This is bound to impede the flow of your work at least slightly, but if you are satisfied that it will enhance your paper, you should have no compunctions about doing so.

If the quotation is only a sentence or two long, you can simply set it off with a colon and quotation marks. If you only want to quote a portion of a sentence, this can also be set off in the same way, and the omitted portion shown by ellipsis points. It is often effective, when quoting only a portion of a sentence, to graft in on to your own sentence. This is called a run-in quotation. For passages that are going to be over four or five lines, you should use a block quotation, in which the passage is single-spaced and given additional indentation. With a block quote, quotation marks are not used, since it is clear from the additional indentation and single spacing that material is being quoted. (Examples of these various kinds of quotations can be seen in the historiographical essay in Chapter Four. Moreover, as you have probably noticed, this book is riddled with block quotes.) A quotation of a page or more, to be used very sparingly, is often best placed as an appendix to your paper.

FOOTNOTING

We can divide our discussion of footnoting into what needs to be footnoted and how it should be done. In regard to the former, most students are fully aware that all quotations must be footnoted; it is the actual footnoting of other material that raises problems. Should each "fact" be footnoted? To do so would be to encumber your text with thick clusters of numbers and a corresponding long list of notes at the bottom of each page (or at the end of the paper, if endnotes are being used). The purpose of footnoting is to allow your reader to check on the accuracy of your quotations, citations, and assertions. You should not footnote a major fact that is well known and unchallenged, such as "President Lincoln was assassinated by John Wilkes Booth" or "The Normans invaded England in 1066." Nor is it necessary to footnote most of those "smaller" facts about events or details in a person's life that the reader can easily check by consulting some of the works in your bibliography. But when such a fact is being emphasized or used for evidence, and certainly when it is in dispute, it needs to be footnoted. Also use a footnote when mentioning another work, primary or secondary, in your text, even if you do not directly quote from it.

There are two basic types of footnotes (or endnotes)—reference footnotes and content footnotes. The former is the documentation of a quotation, citation, or assertion that cites the bibliographic information on the source, including the page number (if applicable). This is the most common type of footnote and your major concern is to format it correctly. There are several major style manuals, and it is important to find out which one (if any) your instructor recommends, and then stick to it consistently. The *Chicago Manual of Style* is the most commonly used in the historical profession,[4] but be sure to check with your instructor. The note format used determines such matters as the manner and sequence in which publication data is stated, how subsequent references to the same work are made, and so on.

The content footnote requires some explanation. One use of it is to provide further elaboration on some point made in a paper, without encumbering the text with a digression that may be of only marginal interest to some readers. Digressions in a story are sometimes unavoidable and can be highly interesting, but if they are employed too much the reader's patience and attention will begin to wane. It is like listening to a long-

---

4 See *The Chicago Manual of Style,* 14th ed. (Chicago: University of Chicago Press, 1993). A shorter, cheaper, and much more convenient reference work for consulting the University of Chicago format is Kate L. Turabian, *A Manual for Writers of Term Papers, Theses, and Dissertations,* Sixth Edition (Chicago: University of Chicago Press, 1996).

winded speaker who insists on giving you a wealth of background detail about each component of his story. We not only grow weary, but such meanderings become so distracting that we lose track of the point and direction of the story. One of the advantages of the written over the spoken word is that such collateral material can be consigned to a content footnote where, perhaps in a few sentences or a paragraph, additional information can be imparted to the reader particularly interested in that point. By using a content footnote correctly, the body of the text is allowed to remain unencumbered.

A similar use of the content footnote is to provide a brief historiographical discussion on some point without cluttering the text. You may, for example, want to relate some fact over which a few scholars are in dispute, or offer differing interpretations. This may be combined with a reference footnote—that is, a citation to a source in your footnote might be immediately followed by something like: "However, this view has recently been challenged by X, who introduces new evidence that casts some doubt on the genuineness of the draft treaty. See . . . ." (here you would have the complete citation to the revisionist article by X).

Whether you are inserting a reference or a content footnote, be sure to use the footnoting function of your word processor. If you neglect to use the footnote command and simply type footnote numbers directly into the text, you will deprive yourself of a very significant advantage of your word processor—its ability to keep track of footnote numbers and the corresponding notes, changing the numbers automatically if you eliminate or rearrange a footnoted passage. None of us with experience of writing in the pre-computer era are likely to forget how quickly manually inserted footnote numbers could get out of sync with the notes, necessitating laborious and time-consuming corrections. Ascertain that the footnote settings on your word processor are correct for the kind of note-footnote or endnote-that you are going to use. Also ensure that you have clicked on the option for Arabic, not Roman numerals (1, 2, 3, not i, ii, iii). And insert the text of the note as soon as the footnote window opens on your screen. If you put that part of the process off until later, you will have to spend additional time finding the book, article, or notecard which you need to cite.[5]

5 What has just been said about the need to use the footnoting system of your word processor can be extended to other functions. Take some time to learn the capabilities of your word-processing application before you start writing—it will pay big dividends. An example is the tendency to use the Tab key or space bar for indenting instead of the formatting commands of the word processing application. When Tab indents or spaces are used, any subsequent change in font, font size, margins, or other formatting features can wreak havoc with the appearance of the text.

Editing and Revising

In striving for excellence in your written work, there is no substitute for painstaking editing and revising. No matter how good you may feel about the quality of your first draft, a later critical scrutiny is certain to reveal inconsistencies, abrupt transitions, unclear passages, infelicitous expressions, and other matters in need of urgent attention. To a lesser degree, the same will apply to a perusal of your second draft, as well as to a third. Rewriting is a critically important phase of the scholarly process, not something that might be squeezed in if you have enough time left before the deadline for submitting your paper. Time is always in short supply for the harried student, so it is essential to plan its use wisely. In addition to leaving time for rewriting, you should, if possible, allow for some "percolation time"—a few days away from research, writing, and rewriting, in which your thoughts can percolate and fresh insights can emerge. It is especially valuable to leave some time between the writing of drafts of your paper and the final version.

In going over your first draft, it is useful to read it aloud. This brings your ear into the process, allowing you to detect more readily those passages that need remedial attention. This is also very helpful in proofreading, because in reading our own work silently, we tend to see what we expect to see, and can easily miss omitted or duplicated letters or words. Having a fellow student listen as you read your work aloud (or read it aloud to you) can also be useful, as long as you have reason to believe that he or she has the ability, interest, and candor to comment critically. Sometimes a senior thesis is taught on a seminar basis, in which portions of rough drafts are read by one's fellow students, who then offer constructive criticism to one another (in addition to that of the instructor). Such encounters almost invariably prove rewarding and interesting, and they create a strong atmosphere of mutual support. These seminars are, or can be, microcosms of the "communities of scholars" that exist in the wider historical profession.

The number of drafts you write will depend on many factors, including your writing abilities, the time at your disposal, and the views of your instructor. Fortunately, the computer has made this part of the writing process immeasurably speedier and more efficient. When the body of your paper is in good shape, you can then turn your attention to revising the introduction and conclusion. Now that the body of your paper is in its finished form, you know exactly what it is that you need to introduce and to conclude.

The introduction should set forth, clearly and briefly, the scope of your paper, the main points to be covered, and a brief statement of your thesis. It is always desirable to engage the reader's attention as quickly as possible, and a well crafted introduction is the key. This may involve the use of a "hook" (a vivid incident illustrative of the events you are about to relate in your paper). It should usually involve a brief historiographic discussion, giving the reader some sense of how the scholarship on your topic has evolved. It should always involve clear sentences, effective structure, and other elements of good writing.

The careful crafting of your conclusion is equally important. Here the emphasis should be on reminding the reader of the main points you have covered, without recapitulating the details of the story. More importantly, here is where you present your overarching conclusion(s) about the material. Don't overreach on the conclusion. Look honestly at the evidence you have marshaled, and ask yourself if it supports the conclusion(s) you have in mind. Remember that most historical evidence is open to a variety of interpretations, some more compelling than others. A sweeping interpretive statement that forecloses all other possibilities may have a resounding ring to it, but is apt to be a red flag to the reader aware of the complexities, ambiguities, and nuances of history. Make your conclusion as strong as the evidence and the structure of your argument warrant, but don't push it beyond that point.

The bibliography, which comes at the very end of the paper, now needs to be added. Like the endnotes (if you are using them rather than footnotes), the bibliography should start on a separate page. Use the page break insert command on your word processor. Your instructor will probably have some guidelines for the bibliography, but it is a common practice to have a list of the primary sources first, followed by a separate listing of the secondary sources. Make sure the entire document is paginated consecutively from the first page of text (page number 1) to the last page of the bibliography. The page number should not be printed on the first page of text, an option built into most word-processing applications. Page numbers should be printed on all other pages (using the pagination command of your word processor), including back matter: endnotes (if these are used instead of footnotes), and the bibliography. Make a final spelling check of the entire document, and then go ahead and print it. An unpaginated cover sheet with your name, the title of your paper, the course, instructor, and date, should also be printed.

One Final Look

Now that you have given the print command and everything seems to be in order, there is a natural desire to get the paper into a nice looking binder and present it to the instructor. Resist the temptation. Treat what you have before you as a final rough draft. If you have a few days before the due date, lay it aside and give yourself a little extra "percolation time." Then go back to it and read it through, carefully and aloud, with a critical eye and ear. You are certain to note some rough spots in the text, and probably some formatting irregularities and other problems. You want to present the very best work you are capable of, and you should also want it to look as good as possible. Taking pride in both the content and appearance of your work is the hallmark of the professional in any field. Do not sell yourself short by neglecting this final opportunity for improvement.

CHAPTER SIX

Conclusion: The Open-ended Nature of History

In legal instruments known as articles of apprenticeship, commonly used in medieval and early modern England, the wording used to refer to an occupation to which a young person was being apprenticed was "art, science, craft, or mystery." This phrase conveys the sense that there were important expressive and creative components to even the most mundane lines of manufacture in the preindustrial age. It is a phrase peculiarly appropriate to the historian's calling. However much the practice of history seems to involve the systematic application of certain skills, there are wide, important areas of both research and writing that call upon the creative spirit. Recall that the Greeks considered history an important enough expressive field to assign one of the nine Muses to it. The modern historical profession still embraces this traditional identification as a branch of literature, even though it often functions in close alliance with the social sciences, or indeed is sometimes classified as one of them. Far from being troubled by their discipline's duality, most historians glory in it. The point is that whether history is viewed as one of the humanities or as one of the social sciences, its creative dimensions are of central importance.

In the sections of this book dealing with research and writing, the emphasis has been on matters that might be considered mechanical in nature—the use of library catalogs, indexes, and various electronic resources, as well as some techniques of reading, notetaking, writing, and revising. One reason for this emphasis is the absolute necessity for students to be well grounded in historical methodology. Another is, quite frankly, that it is much easier to examine systematically the elements of good historical craftsmanship than it is to explain creativity. There are no rules or techniques to being creative, and few creative people in any field can offer much in the way of guidance. Hunches, sudden insights, and inspirations are some of the undoubted manifestations of creativity, but one is tempted to ascribe them to the realm of "mystery," as they did in medieval times.

Nonetheless, even if creativity cannot ultimately be explained, it is possible to recognize it, to encourage it, and to extend it. The first and most essential thing is to discard the notion that a charmed minority of individuals are naturally creative while the rest are forever doomed to being plodders. Whatever mental and psychological processes are involved in creativity, they are, allowing for inevitable differences in capacity and intensity, possessed by everyone. It is possible, of course, for people to convince themselves, or allow others to convince them, that they are somehow deficient in intelligence and imagination. Others may be persuaded that it is not prudent to display any creative qualities. In many societies, past and present, creative impulses are viewed with suspicion, out of fear that they pose a threat to the established order and ways of doing things. Certain religious systems, ideologies, and political programs, insofar as they claim to possess a monopoly of truth, are also inhospitable to the creative spirit. Historical writers with a burning sense of mission to advance particular causes almost invariably subvert the skeptical, open-minded characteristics of the discipline, which are essential if creativity is to flourish. It is a central function of education generally, and of universities in particular, to counteract these baneful tendencies.

One of the best ways historians can aid in this endeavor is to insist on the open-endedness of their discipline. It has been one of the purposes of this book to set forth a view of history as dynamic and evolving. Our views of the past evolve as we move into the future and thus acquire an ever-changing vantage point. Like travelers toiling up the side of a mountain, we find that the configuration of the landscape behind us has changed each time we turn around. Features that were once prominent recede into obscurity while others loom into view, and new patterns and relationships can be discerned. A shifting panorama is, after all, one of the things that makes a journey interesting and instructive. It is all too possible, alas, to take a journey without looking around, or to do so in such a cursory fashion that nothing of significance is detected. No one sets out to write a dull, plodding account; one of the best ways to avoid doing so is to keep in mind that even the smallest project of historical inquiry is part of a larger intellectual odyssey.

My insistence on linking creativity with a conception of history as open-ended perhaps raises the old troubling question about whether or not there is such a thing as objective truth. If "everything is relative," what can we really know about the past? If history is simply a product of the imagination, then is not every person's version as "true" as another's? The answer is a resounding no. Of course there is objective truth in history; it may be elusive but it is usually accessible and must always be rigorously pursued. Truth in history resides in those ascertainable facts that make up the superstructure of any historical account. Whether or not King Harold of England perished at the hands of Norman invaders in the so-called Battle of Hastings in 1066 can be determined by marshaling every fragment of surviving evidence, assessing each source for its authenticity and reliability, and noting inconsistencies and contradictions. The result of this process is an overwhelming conviction that indeed Harold was killed on that fateful October day. His death has become duly registered as one of those countless facts that constitute the annals of the past. Of course, in some sense it, like any fact, must be considered provisional, that is, subject to being changed should contradictory evidence come to light. Nonetheless, it remains a remarkably "sturdy" fact that, like the vast majority of other verifiable occurrences, will almost certainly not be altered. Thus we can rest assured that these verified past events will not be plucked away or overturned by whim or fancy.

However, the broad array of widely accepted facts, contrary to popular belief, does not constitute history. History is the intellectual discipline that, in addition to discovering, verifying, and describing past events, imposes pattern and meaning upon them. Indeed, the imposing of pattern and meaning, and the discerning of processes, are the most important parts of the historian's calling. It is here that creativity flourishes. Here, too, is the arena in which historians offer fresh approaches, new methodologies, and sometimes major revisionist interpretations. If history is conceived as a fixed chronicle, there is little scope for either creativity or revisionism, which march hand in hand. They must continue to do so if history is to respond to the changing needs and aspirations of the ever-advancing present, as well as to provide thoughtful anticipation of the future.

Published Bibliographies

Guide to Reference Books. Edited by Robert Balay. 11th ed. Chicago: American Library Association, 1996. In the section on history, this guide lists numerous bibliographies and other reference materials (atlases, chronologies, etc.) for all facets of historical study.

Bibliographies in History. Foreword by Eric H. Boehm. 2 vols. Santa Barbara: ABC-Clio, 1988. Volume 1 lists published bibliographies on U.S. and Canadian history; volume 2 covers all other countries.

American Historical Association Guide to Historical Literature. Edited by Mary Beth Norton. 3rd ed., 2 vols. New York: Oxford University Press, 1995. An excellent guide to essential books, articles, and essays in all fields of history.

Harvard Guide to American History. Edited by Frank Freidel. Rev. ed. Cambridge, Mass: Belknap Press, 1974. Though a bit dated, this is still a useful guide to both primary and secondary sources.

Historiography: An Annotated Bibliography of Journal Articles, Books, and *Dissertations.* Edited by Susan K. Kinnell. 2 vols. Santa Barbara: ABC-Clio, 1987.

People in World History: An Index to Biographies in History Journals and Dissertations in All Countries of the World except the U.S. and Canada. Edited by Susan K. Kinnell. 2 vols. Santa Barbara: ABC-Clio, 1988. A very full and useful index by occupation, region or country, as well as surname.

People in History: An Index to U.S. and Canadian Biographies in History Journals and Dissertations. Edited by Susan K. Kinnell. 2 vols. Santa Barbara: ABC-Clio, 1988. A very full and useful index by occupation, region, and surname.

Reference Sources in History: an Introductory Guide. Edited by Ronald H. Fritze, Brian E. Coutts, and Louis A. Vyhnanek. Santa Barbara: ABC-Clio, 1990. Helpful guide to a wide range of reference materials in History.

Major Databases for Bibliographic Searching

The following are widely available, most of them in both online and published form, a few only in published volumes. New databases are certain to be added, while others are apt to undergo at least partial name changes. You should always explore any interesting sounding database in your quest for sources.

WorldCat
ArticleFirst
Humanities Index (called *Humanities Full Text* in its online form)
Social Sciences Index (called *Social Sciences Full Text* in its online form)
Essay and General Literature Index
Historical Abstracts
America: History and Life
Academic Search Elite
World History Full Text
OmniFile Full Text Mega
J-Stor
NetFirst
Dissertation Abstracts International
Hispanic American Periodicals Index
British Humanities Index

Footnote/Endnote Formatting

The following employs University of Chicago style, the most commonly used in the historical profession. These examples cover the great majority of citations required. For other cases, consult the *Chicago Manual of Style*.[1]

BOOKS

A book citation in a footnote/endnote requires: a) author's name (first name first) as given on the title page; b) full title (including subtitle, if any); c) place of publication, publisher, and date in parentheses; d) page number(s) of the specific citation, unless it is the entire work rather than some part that is being cited. In addition, if the book cited is an edition other than the first, this must be indicated following the title (e.g. "2d ed."). If no place of publication or date of publication is given, insert "n.p." or "n.d." In a multivolume work, the volume number must be indicated just prior to the page numbers if it is to a specific part of the work. If the citation is to the entire work, give the number of volumes (e.g., "3 vols.") immediately after the title. Page number citations for books are not preceded by "p." or "pp." Titles of books are always italicized, not placed in quotation marks.

---

1 14th ed. (Chicago: University of Chicago Press, 1993). The most convenient source for looking up all aspects of University of Chicago format is that paperback classic, Kate L. Turabian *A Manual for Writers of Term Papers, Theses, and Dissertations,* 6th ed. (Chicago: University of Chicago Press, 1996). Make certain that you consult the most recent edition of either the *Chicago Manual of Style* or the Turabian book.

Book by a single author:
1. Andrew Cunningham McLaughlin, *America and Britain* (New York: E.P. Dutton, 1919), 137.

Book by two authors:
2. Fritz M. Heichelheim and Cedric A. Yeo, *A History of the Roman People* (Englewood Cliffs, NJ: Prentice-Hall, 1962), 296.

Book by three authors:
3. Richard Hofstadter, William Miller, and Daniel Aaron, *The American Republic (*Englewood Cliffs, NJ: Prentice-Hall, 1959), Vol. 2, 391.
[NB: this is also an example of a specific citation within one volume of a multivolume work]

Book by four or more authors:
4. James Henretta and others, *America's History,* 4th ed., 2 vols. (New York and Boston: Bedford/St. Martin's, 2000).
[NB: this is an example of a citation to an entire multivolume work; it is also an example of a citation to a later edition]

Book with author(s) as editor(s):
5. Donald T. Critchlow and Charles H. Parker, eds., *With Us Always: Private Charity and Public Assistance in Historical Perspective,* (Lanham, MD: Rowman and Littlefield, 1998).
[NB: this is how to cite an entire book of essays (chapters) written by various authors. The proper formatting for citing the individual essays within is given below under Essay (Chapter)]

ARTICLES AND ESSAYS (CHAPTERS)

The formatting of authors' names, including multiple authors, is the same as for books. The titles of articles are always in quotation marks and not italicized. The names of journals and other periodicals are italicized. The volume number of a journal follows immediately after the journal name, without "vol.," "v.," or other such designations. This is followed by the date of that issue of the journal in parentheses. A colon and page numbers follow the date and are inclusive of the entire article if that is being cited. If just a portion of the article is being cited, only that page number (or those page numbers) should follow.

Journal Article:
6. Thomas Benjamin, "A Time of Reconquest: History, the Maya Revival, and the Zapatista Rebellion in Chiapas," *American Historical Review* 105 (April 2000): 417–50.
[NB: this is a citation to an entire article. If only a portion of the article is being cited, just give that page or page range]

Magazine Article:
7. Bruce Bower, "Trailing Lewis and Clark," *Science News,* Sept. 26, 1998, 205.

Newspaper Article:
8. Patt Morrison, "France and California: Vive the Differences and Similarities," *Los Angeles Times,* June 20, 2001, Sec. B, p. 3.
[NB: If no author is given, just provide the other information]

Encyclopedia Article:
Signed article:
9. Peter N. Stearns, "Social History," in *A Global Encyclopedia of Historical Writing.*
Unsigned article:
10. *The New Century Classical Handbook,* s.v. "Golden Apples of the Hesperides."

Essay (Chapter):
11. Anthony Brundage, "Private Charity and the 1834 Poor Law," in *With Us Always: Private Charity and Public Assistance in Historical Perspective,* ed. Donald T. Critchlow and Charles H. Parker (Lanham, MD: Rowman and Littlefield, 1998), 108.

Book Review:
12. Lesley Abrams, review of *Kingship and Government in Pre-Conquest England, c. 500–1066,* by Ann Williams, *Albion* 32 (Fall 2000): 467.

OTHER TYPES OF SOURCES

Dissertation:
13. Michael Steven Smith, "Anti-Radical Expression: Counter-Revolutionary Thought in the Age of Revolution" (Ph.D. diss., University of California, Riverside, 1999), 132.

Government Document:
14. United States Commission on Civil Rights, *Civil Rights '63: 1963 Report of the United States Commission on Civil Rights* (Washington: GPO, 1963), 209.

Web Site:
15. Lynn McDonald, "Collected Works of Florence Nightingale: Introduction to the Project," 1998, accessed 21 June 2001; available from http://www.anthropology.uoguelph.ca/fnightingale/introduction.htm; Internet.

Videorecording:
16. *The Architecture of Frank Lloyd Wright,* prod. Barbara and Murray Grigor, writ. and dir. Murray Grigor, 75 min., Direct Cinema Limited, 1993, videocassette.

Footnote Reference to a Previously Cited Work

When making a subsequent citation to a work previously cited in an earlier footnote/endnote, do not repeat all the information. Use a short form, the simplest of which is the author's surname followed by the page reference. If, however, there is more than one work by that author in your bibliography, you need to add a short version of the title. If you had already cited, say, Stephen E. Ambrose's book, *Undaunted Courage: Meriwether Lewis, Thomas Jefferson, and the Opening of the American West,* then you would not have to repeat all this, or the publication data, in a subsequent note. Assuming that there were no other works by this author in your bibliography, you could cite it the following way:

17. Ambrose, 193.

If you had another work by Ambrose in your bibliography, you would need:

18. Ambrose, *Undaunted Courage,* 193.

If there was another author in your bibliography with the same surname, you would need to provide the first name in order to avoid confusion. It is also acceptable to use "Ibid." (short for the Latin word *ibidem,* meaning "in the same place," but only when the footnote/endnote reference follows a full citation of that work in the **immediately** preceding note. For example:

19. Stephen E. Ambrose, *Undaunted Courage: Meriwether Lewis, Thomas Jefferson, and the Opening of the American West* (New York: Simon and Schuster, 1996), 88.
20. Ibid., 193.

Bibliography Formatting

The key to understanding bibliography formatting is that materials are organized alphabetically, usually by authors' surnames. When there are two or more works by one author, ordinarily the alphabetization of the titles will determine the order in which to list them. In such cases, the author's name is listed only for the first entry. For the following entries by that author, the name is replaced by underscoring (see sample bibliography).

Book:
McLaughlin, Andrew Cunningham. *America and Britain.* New York: E.P. Dutton, 1919.

Article:
Benjamin, Thomas. "A Time of Reconquest: History, the Maya Revival, and the Zapatista Rebellion in Chiapas." *American Historical Review* 105 (April 2000): 417–50.

Essay (Chapter):
Brundage, Anthony. "Private Charity and the 1834 Poor Law." In *With Us Always: Private Charity and Public Assistance in Historical Perspective,* ed. Donald T. Critchlow and Charles H. Parker, 99–119. Lanham, MD: Rowman and Littlefield, 1998.

Dissertation:
Smith, Michael Steven. "Anti-Radical Expression: Counter-Revolutionary Thought in the Age of Revolution." Ph.D. diss., University of California, Riverside, 1999.

Sample Bibliography:
Bibliography entries are single-spaced, with subsequent lines indented. A period, not a comma, should follow authors' names as well as the titles of the works. Unlike footnotes/endnotes, parentheses are not used to enclose place of publication, publisher, and date. The following shows secondary sources. In a research paper, primary sources are generally listed separately, and appear before the secondary sources. Primary sources in the form of books, articles, and chapters follow the same rules as those for secondary materials.

Anstruther, Ian. *The Scandal of the Andover Workhouse.* 2d ed. Gloucester: Sutton, 1984.

Apfel, William, and Peter Dunkley. "English Rural Society and the New Poor Law: Bedfordshire, 1834–1847." *Social History* 10 (1985): 37–68.

Bartlett, Peter. "The Asylum, the Workhouse, and the Voice of the Insane Poor in 19th-Century England." *International Journal of Law and Psychiatry* 21 (1998): 421–32.

Brundage, Anthony. *The English Poor Laws, 1700–1930.* New York: Palgrave, 2002.

———. "Reform of the Poor Law Electoral System, 1834–1894." *Albion* 7 (1975): 201–15.

Choomwattana, Chakrit. "The opposition to the New Poor Law in Sussex, 1834–1837." Ph.D. diss., Cornell University, 1986.

Cody, Lisa Forman. "The Politics of Illegitimacy in an Age of Reform: Women, Reproduction, and Political Economy in England's New Poor Law of 1834." *Journal of Women's History* 11 (2000): 131–56.

Daunton, M. J. *Progress and Poverty: An Economic and Social History of Britain, 1700–1850.* Oxford: Oxford University Press, 1995.

Fido, Judith. "The Charity Organisation Society and Social Casework in London 1869–1900." In *Social Control in Nineteenth Century Britain,* ed. A. P. Donajgrodzki, 207–30. London: Croom Helm, 1977.

Franzén, Katharine Mary Grigsby. "Free to leave: government assisted emigration under the 1834 Poor Law." Ph.D. diss., University of Virginia, 1996.

Huzel, James P. "The Labourer and the Poor Law, 1750–1850." In *The Agrarian History of England and Wales, Vol. VI, 1750–1850,* ed. G.E. Mingay, 755–810. Cambridge: Cambridge University Press, 1989.

Jones, Margaret. "The 1908 Old Age Pensions Act: The Poor Law in New Disguise?" In *Social Conditions, Status, and Community, 1860– c.1920,* ed. Keith Laybourn, 82–103. Stroud: Sutton, 1997.

Landau, Norma. "The Eighteenth–Century Context of the Laws of Settlement." *Continuity and Change* 6 (1991): 417–39.

Lees, Lynn Hollen. *The Solidarities of Strangers: The English Poor Laws and the People, 1700–1948.* Cambridge: Cambridge University Press, 1998.

———. "The Survival of the Unfit: Welfare Policies and Family Maintenance in Nineteenth-Century London." In *The Uses of Charity: The Poor on Relief in the Nineteenth-Century Metropolis,* ed. Peter Mandler, 68–91. Philadelphia: University of Pennsylvania Press, 1990.

Levine-Clark, Marjorie. "Engendering Relief: Women, Ablebodiedness, and the New Poor Law in Early Victorian England." *Journal of Women's History* 11 (2000): 107–30.

Melling, Joseph, Richard Adair, and Bill Forsythe. "'A Proper Lunatic for Two Years': Pauper Lunatic Children in Victorian and Edwardian England: Child Admissions to the Devon County Asylum, 1845–1914." *Journal of Social History* 31 (1997): 371–405.

Poynter, J. R. *Society and Pauperism: English Ideas on Poor Relief, 1795–1834.* London: Routledge & Kegan Paul, 1969.

Richardson, Ruth. *Death, Dissection, and the Destitute.* London: Routledge & Kegan Paul, 1987.

Rose, Mary Beth. "Social Policy and Business: Parish Apprenticeship and the Factory System, 1750–1834." *Business History* 31 (1989): 5–32.

Song, Byung Khun. "Agrarian Policies on Pauper Settlement and Migration, Oxfordshire, 1750–1834." *Continuity and Change* 13, (1998): 363–89.

———. "Continuity and Change in English Rural Society: The Formation of Poor Law Unions in Oxfordshire." *English Historical Review* 114 (1999): 314–38.

———. "Landed Interest, Local Government, and the Labour Market in England, 1750–1850." *Economic History Review* 51 (1998): 465–88.

Vorspan, Rachel. "Vagrancy and the New Poor Law in Late Victorian and Edwardian England." *English Historical Review* 92 (1977): 59–81.

Webb, Sidney, and Beatrice Webb. *English Poor Law History. Part II: The Last Hundred Years.* 2 vols. London: Longmans Green, 1929.

Winch, Donald. *Riches and Poverty: An Intellectual History of Political Economy in Britain, 1750–1834.* Cambridge: Cambridge University Press, 1996.

Commonly Used Abbreviations

anon.	anonymous
app.	appendix
art.	article
b.	born
c.	copyright
ca.	*circa,* around, approximately, as in ca. 1834
cf.	*confer,* compare, a suggestion that the reader compare two or more works
ch. or chap.	chapter (plural, chaps.)
col.	column (plural, cols.)
d.	died
diss.	dissertation
e.g.	*exempli gratia,* for example
et al.	*et alia,* and others
et seq.	*et sequentes,* and the following
fig.	figure
fl.	*floruit,* used when birth and death dates are unknown
ibid.	*ibidem,* in the same place
id.	*idem,* the same person, usually referring to an author
i.e.	*id est,* that is
ill.	illustrated or illustration
infra	below, a reference to a later point in the work
l. or ll.	line or lines
n.	footnote or endnote (plural, nn.)
n.d.	no date of publication provided
no.	number
n.p.	no place of publication or no publisher provided
n.s.	new series

op. cit.	*opere citato,* in the work cited
o.s.	old series
p.	page (plural, pp.)
par.	paragraph (plural, pars.)
passim	here and there throughout the work
pseud.	pseudonym
pt.	part (plural, pts.)
q.v.	*quod vide,* which see, indicating a cross reference
rev.	revised
sec.	section
sic	so, thus, placed in brackets following an obvious error, misspelling, etc. in a quotation to indicate that it indeed appears that way in the original
supp. or suppl.	supplement
supra	above, a reference to an earlier point in the work
s.v.	*sub verbo,* under the word, referring to an encyclopedia entry
trans.	translator or translated by
viz.	*videlicet,* namely
vol. or v.	volume

Suggestions for
Further Reading ◆◆◆◆

The following short list of books represents only a small portion of the many valuable texts and reference works that might be of service to students of history. Each book is apt to prove valuable for different aspects of research and writing.

Appleby, Joyce, Lynn Hunt, and Margaret Jacob. *Telling the Truth about History.* New York and London: W. W. Norton & Co., 1995. An incisive analysis of the impact of scientific thinking and the concept of objectivity on historians in the modern era; this work includes a thoughtful discussion of postmodernism's challenge to modern historiography.

Barzun, Jacques, and Henry Graff. *The Modern Researcher.* 6th ed. Fort Worth: Harcourt College Publishers, 2002. A classic in the field, this lengthy, well-written guide by two masters of the historian's craft is particularly useful for its exploration of the intellectual processes involved in researching and writing history.

Breisach, Ernst. *Historiography, Ancient, Medieval, and Modern.* 2d ed. Chicago: University of Chicago Press, 1994. An excellent survey text of the history of history writing from the ancient world to the twentieth century.

Conkin, Paul K., and Roland H. Stromberg. *Heritage and Challenge: The History and Theory of History.* Wheeling, Ill.: Harlan Davidson, Inc., 1989. Combines a brief yet scholarly history of historical writing with a concise, sophisticated analysis of the major philosophical and theoretical issues confronting historians today.

Furay, Conal, and Michael J. Salevouris. *The Methods and Skills of History: A Practical Guide.* 2d ed. Wheeling, Ill.: Harlan Davidson,

Inc., 2000. A good methods text/workbook that combines theory with "hands on" practice.

Gilderhus, Mark T. *History and Historians: A Historiographical Introduction.* 4th ed. Englewood Cliffs, N.J.: Prentice-Hall, 1999. A concise, lucid introduction to the history of history writing as well as some of the basics of research.

Mann, Thomas. *A Guide to Library Research Methods.* New York: Oxford University Press, 1990. A detailed exploration of various research strategies and resources.

Storey, William Kelleher. *Writing History: A Guide for Students.* New York: Oxford University Press, 1999. Effective guide to research and writing with especially good sections on making inferences from primary sources, narrative techniques, editing, and revising.

Strunk, William Jr., and E. B. White. *The Elements of Style.* 4th ed. Boston: Allyn & Bacon, 2000. A classic in its own right that explores the subject of style, urging and helping the reader to write with wit, verve, and clarity. A particularly good guide to commonly misused words and phrases.

Turabian, Kate L. *A Manual for Writers of Term Papers, Theses, and Dissertations.* 6th ed. Chicago: University of Chicago Press, 1996. Based on the University of Chicago *Manual of Style*, this short reference work covers all aspects of citing and formatting, not just for history and the social sciences but for other fields as well.

Index ◆◆◆◆